How to Use this Book

Matched to the National Curriculum, this Collins Year 3 Reading Comprehension workbook is designed to improve comprehension skills.

Diverse and engaging texts including **fiction**, **non-fiction** and **poetry**.

Tests **increase in difficulty** as you work through the book.

Bill's New Frock

When Bill Simpson woke up on Monday morning, he found he was a girl.

He was still standing staring at himself in the mirror, quite baffled, when his mother swept in.

'Why don't you wear this pretty pink dress?' she said.

'I never wear dresses,' Bill burst out.

'I know,' his mother said. 'It's such a pity.'

And, to his astonishment, before he could even begin to argue, she had dropped the dress over his head and zipped up the back.

'I'll leave you to do up the shell buttons,' she said. 'They're a bit fiddly and I'm late for work.'

And she swept out, leaving him staring in dismay at the mirror. In it, a girl with his curly red hair and wearing a pretty pink frock with fiddly shell buttons was staring back at him in equal dismay.

'This can't be true,' Bill Simpson said to himself. 'This cannot be true!'

He stepped out of his bedroom just as his father was rushing past. He, too, was late in getting off to work.

Mr Simpson leaned over and planted a kiss on Bill's cheek.

'Bye, Poppet,' he said, ruffling Bill's curls. 'You look very sweet today. It's not often we see you in a frock, is it?'

He ran down the stairs and out of the house so quickly he didn't see Bill's scowl, or hear what he muttered savagely under his breath.

by Anne Fine

Challenge 1

1. '…staring in dismay in the mirror.' Circle the word below that is closest in meaning to 'dismay'.

   alarm   disgust   joy   excitement   1 mark

2. Find and copy a word with a similar meaning to 'dress'. _____   1 mark

3. What colour is Bill's hair? _____   1 mark

26

Challenge 2

1. Give two reasons why the word 'never' is in italics.

   _____   2 marks

2. Why do you think Bill keeps staring in the mirror?

   _____   1 mark

3. '…his mother swept in.'

   a) What does the word 'swept' suggest about the way Bill's mother was moving?   1 mark

   b) Why do you think she is moving like this?   1 mark

Challenge 3

1. Do you think Bill's parents were surprised he was a girl? Give a reason for your answer.   2 marks

2. At the start of the extract, Bill feels 'baffled'. How have his feelings changed by the end of the extract?   1 mark

3. What do you think might happen next in the story? Explain your prediction.   2 marks

Total: _____ / 13 marks

😕 Had a go ☐   🙂 Getting there ☐   😀 Got it! ☐

27

Questions split into three levels of difficulty – **Challenge 1**, **Challenge 2** and **Challenge 3** – to help progression.

Total marks boxes for recording progress and '**How am I doing**' checks for self-evaluation.

Starter test recaps skills covered in Year 2.

Three **Progress tests** included throughout the book for ongoing assessment and monitoring progress.

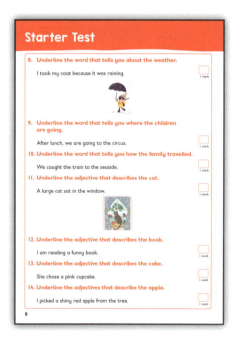

Answers provided for all the questions.

Contents

How to Use This Book		1
Reading Comprehension at Home		4
Starter Test		**6**
The Enchanting Song of the Magical Bird by Nelson Mandela	Fiction	14
A Dragonfly by Eleanor Farjeon	Poetry	16
A Book of Bears by Katie Viggers	Non-fiction	18
The Sheep-Pig by Dick King-Smith	Fiction	20
The Magnificent Bull by Fiona Waters (from Dinka poem, translator unknown)	Poetry	22
Who Are You Calling Weird? by Marilyn Singer	Non-fiction	24
Bill's New Frock by Anne Fine	Fiction	26
Making Mistakes by Daniel Thompson	Poetry	28
The Magic and Mystery of Trees by Jen Green	Non-fiction	30
Progress Test 1		**32**
The Magic Finger by Roald Dahl	Fiction	36
Grrrr by Francesca Beard	Poetry	39
Africa, Amazing Africa: Country by Country by Atinuke	Non-fiction	42
Mr Majeika by Humphrey Carpenter	Fiction	45
The Princess's Treasures by Clare Bevan	Poetry	48

Recipe for Fire by Mark Brake	Non-fiction	**51**
Progress Test 2		**54**
Stuart Little by E.B. White	Fiction	**58**
Cinderella by Roald Dahl	Poetry	**62**
How to be a Scientist by Steve Mould	Non-fiction	**66**
Mindy Kim and the Yummy Seaweed Business by Lyla Lee	Fiction	**70**
Taking out the Tigers by Brian Moses	Poetry	**74**
What is Science?	Non-fiction	**78**
The Lion, the Witch and the Wardrobe by C.S. Lewis	Fiction	**82**
Progress Test 3		**86**
Answers		**90**

Acknowledgments

The author and publisher are grateful to the copyright holders for permission to use quoted materials and images.

THE LION, THE WITCH AND THE WARDROBE by C.S. Lewis copyright © C.S. Lewis Pte. Ltd. 1950. Extract reprinted by permission; Illustration by Pauline Baynes copyright© C.S. Lewis Pte. Ltd. 1950. Reprinted by permission; The Boy at the Back of the Class by Onjali Rauf reproduced by permission of Orion Children's Books, an imprint of Hachette Children's Books, Carmelite House, 50 Victoria Embankment, London imprint, EC4Y 0DZ; 'Making Mistakes' a poem from the book 'Big Thoughts for Little Thinkers' by Daniel Thompson reproduced with permission; Aye Aye in 'Who Are You Calling Weird?', written by Marilyn Singer and illustrated by Paul Daviz, published by words & pictures, an imprint of The Quarto Group, copyright © 2018. Reproduced by permission of Quarto Publishing Plc; A Dragonfly by Eleanor Farjeon reproduced with permission from David Higham; A Martian in the Supermarket by Penelope Lively reproduced with permission from David Higham; A Bear Called Paddington by Michael Bond. Reproduced by permission of The Agency (London) Ltd © Michael Bond 1958. US rights by permission of the Estate of Michael Bond. Bill's New Frock reprinted by permission of HarperCollins Publishers Ltd © (2007) Anne Fine. The Princess's Treasures was taken from Princess Poems by Clare Bevan, published by Macmillan. © Clare Bevan, 2005; Mr Majeika by Humphrey Carpenter, published by Puffin, a division of Penguin Random House. © Humphrey Carpenter, 1985; Africa, Amazing Africa: Country by Country by Atinuke, published by Walker Book. © Atinuke, 2019; GRRRR by Francesca Beard is used by permission of the author. © Francesca Beard, 2009; The Magic Finger by Roald Dahl, published by Puffin Books, a division of Penguin Random House. © Roald Dahl;

The Ghost Teacher was taken from Heard it in the Playground by Allan Ahlberg. Published by Puffin Books, a division of Penguin Random House. © Allan Ahlberg, 1991; The Magic and Mystery of Trees by Jen Green, published by DK Children's. ©Jen Green, 2019; The Magnificent Bull by The Dinka people of Africa, was taken from: Tiger Tiger Burning Bright, published by Nosy Crow; The Sheep-Pig by Dick King-Smith. Published by Puffin Books, a division of Penguin Random House. © Dick King-Smith, 2019; A Book of Bears by Katie Viggers, published by: Laurence King Publishing. © Katie Viggers, 2018; Cinderella was taken from Revolting Rhymes by Roald Dahl. Published by Puffin Books, a division of Penguin Random House. © Roald Dahl, 1982; Stuart Little by EB White, published by Puffin Books, a division of Penguin Random House. © EB White, 1945; The Enchanting Song of the Magical Bird was taken from: Nelson Mandela's Favorite African Folktales by Nelson Mandela; Nim's Island by Wendy Orr ©Wendy Orr, 2008. Published by Puffin Books, a division of Penguin Random House; Working in Space was taken from First Space Encyclopedia, published by DK Children's; What is Science? was taken from Science Encyclopedia, published by National Geographic Kids; Tree was taken from The Time-Travelling Underpants by James Carter. © James Carter, 2007. Published by Macmillan and used by permission; Amazing Tales of the World's Greatest Adventurers by Nellie Huang, © Nellie Huang, 2019. Published by DK Children's; Mindy Kim and the Yummy Seaweed Business by Lyla Lee © Lyla Lee, 2020. Published by Aladdin, a division of Simon & Schuster; Taking out the Tigers was taken from: Lost Magic: The Very Best of Brian Moses by Brian Moses, © 2017. Published by Macmillan Books and used by permission; Recipe for Fire was taken from The Big Earth Book by Mark Brake. © Mark Brake, 2017. Published by Lonely Planet Kids; How to be a Scientist by Steve Mould © Steve Mould, 2017. Published by DK Children's.

All illustrations and images are ©Shutterstock.com and ©HarperCollins Publishers Ltd.

Published by Collins
An imprint of HarperCollins Publishers
1 London Bridge Street
London SE1 9GF

HarperCollins Publishers
1st Floor, Watermarque Building,
Ringsend Road, Dublin 4, Ireland

© HarperCollins Publishers Limited 2021

ISBN 978-0-00-846757-9

First published 2021

10 9 8 7 6 5 4 3 2 1

British Library Cataloguing in Publication Data.

A CIP record of this book is available from the British Library.

Publisher: Fiona McGlade
Author: Alison Head
Copyeditor: Fiona Watson
Project Management: Shelley Teasdale
Cover Design: Sarah Duxbury
Inside Concept Design and Page Layout: Ian Wrigley
Production: Karen Nulty
Printed in the United Kingdom by Martins the Printers

Reading Comprehension at Home

These activities can be easily carried out at home when reading for pleasure with your child, or when your child is reading for pleasure on their own. They will help build your child's comprehension skills and are fun to do.

Poets corner

Help your child to develop their understanding of a character from a story they are reading by encouraging them to write an acrostic poem, where each line of the poem begins with the next letter in the character's name. Help them to think of an appropriate adjective for each letter of the character's name that describes something about them.

What happens next?

When you are reading a story or narrative poem with your child, stop at a suitable point in the story and ask them to predict what will happen next, and to explain why they think that. Encourage them to think about how their understanding of the characters and the events so far helped them with their prediction.

Word families

When you are reading with your child, take the time to explore the meaning of unfamiliar words to ensure they understand what they have read. Encourage them to use the context to help them work out what new words mean, and to use a dictionary to double-check the meaning. Make a note of familiar words that have similar meanings to develop their understanding.

Picture perfect

When you are reading non-fiction with your child, consider the pictures, diagrams and charts that have been included, as well as the words. Discuss why you think those particular pictures, diagrams and charts were chosen, and how they help the reader to understand the text. Ask them to suggest other artwork they would like to see included on the page.

Act it out!

Try acting out stories your child enjoys. This could be as simple as creating different voices for each character as you read the story, or you could develop it into a whole performance, with costumes and props. Encourage your child to take the lead and see where their imagination takes them!

Make connections

When you are reading with your child, encourage them to make connections between the book and their own experiences. For example, you may want to ask them if they remember a time when they had a similar experience to a character in the book; if they can think of other poems with similar characters, settings or themes; or if they've seen or heard about the information you read in a non-fiction book.

Join the library

Borrowing books from your local library is an easy and inexpensive way to ensure that your child experiences a wide range of books. Children's librarians are experts at ensuring their collections are full of well-loved classics, new releases, comics, audio stories and interesting non-fiction. Many local libraries also run story sessions and arrange activity sessions aimed at encouraging reading.

Words in focus

Give your child time to work on words they find difficult to read. Don't be too quick to read it for them, but show them strategies they could use, for example breaking it down into syllables. Make sure your child understands the meaning of the word before moving on.

Starter Test

1. **Draw a line to match up the pairs of words that are similar in meaning.**

   merry   riches

   giant   good

   treasure   huge

   beautiful   jolly

   kind   attractive

2. **Circle four things in the box that you might find in a fairy tale.**

a dinosaur	a castle	a lorry
	a fairy	a witch
a space man	a princess	a school

Look at this contents page from a non-fiction book about sports.

Contents

Football	6
Netball	8
Cricket	11
Rugby	14
Basketball	15

3. **What page would you look at to read about cricket?**

....

1 mark

4. **What sport would you read about on page 15?**

....

1 mark

5. **How many pages are there about netball?**

....

1 mark

6. **Which sport has only one page about it?**

....

1 mark

7. **If you were reading this book, which page would you want to read first, and why?**

....

....

1 mark

Starter Test

8. **Underline the word that tells you about the weather.**

    I took my coat because it was raining.

    1 mark

9. **Underline the word that tells you where the children are going.**

    After lunch, we are going to the circus.

    1 mark

10. **Underline the word that tells you how the family travelled.**

    We caught the train to the seaside.

    1 mark

11. **Underline the adjective that describes the cat.**

    A large cat sat in the window.

    1 mark

12. **Underline the adjective that describes the book.**

    I am reading a funny book.

    1 mark

13. **Underline the adjective that describes the cake.**

    She chose a pink cupcake.

    1 mark

14. **Underline the adjectives that describe the apple.**

    I picked a shiny red apple from the tree.

    1 mark

Choose words from the box that you would find in each place listed in the table. Write the words in the table.

television	elephant	swings
tiger	slide	roundabout
sofa	chair	camel

15.	At the zoo		
16.	At the playground		
17.	In the living room		

9 marks

Add a word that could be used to complete each sentence so that it makes sense.

18. I made a _____ cake.

1 mark

19. We caught the _____ to town.

1 mark

20. They _____ the road carefully.

1 mark

Starter Test

Paddington Goes Underground by **Michael Bond**

Paddington was very surprised when he woke up and found himself in bed. He decided it was a nice feeling as he stretched himself and pulled the sheets up round his head with a paw. He reached out with his feet and found a cool spot for his toes. One advantage of being a very small bear in a large bed was that there was so much room.

After a few minutes he poked his head out cautiously and sniffed. There was a lovely smell of something coming under the door. It seemed to be getting nearer and nearer. There were footsteps too, coming up the stairs.

21. How big is Paddington? Tick your answer.

very small ☐   very large ☐

1 mark

22. '...he poked his head out cautiously...' Circle the word that is closest in meaning to 'cautiously'.

carefully   **slowly**   **sadly**   **boldly**

1 mark

23. What do you think Paddington could smell?

....

1 mark

24. Why do you think the smell got 'nearer and nearer'?

....

1 mark

Recycling

We throw a lot of rubbish away! Think about all of the packaging that your food and drink comes in, the toys you do not play with anymore, and the clothes you have outgrown. What happens to it all?

The best solution is to find ways to create less rubbish, but we are also making better use of the rubbish we do make, by recycling it into new things. We can turn old magazines and cardboard boxes into new paper and card, and old plastic bottles into new ones, or even into fleece clothing!

What things do you recycle at home?

25. Give one example from the text of something people throw away.

....

1 mark

26. What word is used to mean that you have grown too big for your clothes?

....

1 mark

27. Name one good thing we can do with our rubbish.

....

1 mark

28. Find two things that can be made from recycled plastic bottles.

.... and ....

2 marks

29. What reason does the text give to explain why people might throw toys away?

....

1 mark

Starter Test

> **At the Seaside** by Robert Louis Stevenson
>
> When I was down beside the sea
>
> A wooden spade they gave to me
>
> To dig the sandy shore.
>
> My holes were empty like a cup.
>
> In every hole the sea came up
>
> Till it could come no more.

30. What was the spade in the poem made of?

....

1 mark

31. Circle the word below that is not similar in meaning to the word 'shore'.

    beach   **sands**   **bank**   **coast**

1 mark

32. Do you think the narrator of the poem was a child or an adult? Give a reason for your answer.

....

....

2 marks

33. Who do you think might have given the narrator the spade?

....

1 mark

34. 'In every hole the sea came up

    Till it could come no more.'

    Why could the sea not come up into the holes anymore?

....

1 mark

A Martian in the Supermarket by Penelope Lively

It was the middle of the night when the rocket landed in the supermarket car-park. The engine had failed. The hatch opened and the Martian peered out. A Martian, I should tell you, is about three feet high and has webbed feet, green skin and eyes on the ends of horns like a snail. This one, who was three hundred and twenty-seven years old, wore a red jersey.

He said "Bother!" He had only passed his driving test the week before and was always losing his way. He was an extremely nervous person, and felt the cold badly. He shivered. A car hooted and he scuttled behind a rubbish bin. Everything looked very strange and frightening.

35. **Find and copy the adjective that is used to describe the Martian's feet.** ....

I mark

36. **How old was the Martian? Circle your answer.**

3 years old   300 years old

327 years old   27 years old

I mark

37. **The Martian 'wore a red jersey'. What is another word with a similar meaning to 'jersey'?** ....

I mark

38. **How do you think the Martian is feeling? Give a reason for your answer.**

....

....

2 marks

39. **Do you think the Martian had landed on Earth before? Give a reason for your answer.**

....

....

2 marks

Total: _____ /56 marks

The Enchanting Song of the Magical Bird

One day, a strange bird arrived in a small village that nestled among low hills. From that moment on, nothing was safe. Anything the villagers planted in the fields disappeared overnight. Every morning there were fewer and fewer sheep and goats and chickens. Even during the day, while the people were working on the lands, the gigantic bird would come and break open their storehouses and granaries, and steal from them their winter food supplies.

The villagers were devastated. There was misery in the land – everywhere was the sound of wailing and the gnashing of teeth. No one – not even the bravest hero of the village – could get his hands on the bird. It was just too quick for them. They hardly ever saw it: they just heard the rushing of its great wings as it came to perch in the crown of the old yellowwood tree, under its thick canopy of leaves.

by Nelson Mandela

Challenge 1

1 '…a small village that nestled among low hills.' Circle the word below that is similar in meaning to 'nestled'.

   built   **lived**   **huddled**   **grew**

   ☐ 1 mark

2 Find and copy two pieces of evidence that tell you that the bird was very big.

   _____

   ☐ 2 marks

3 What does the word 'devastated' suggest about how the villagers felt about their food being stolen?

   _____

   ☐ 1 mark

Challenge 2

1 What animals did the villagers keep?

....

☐ 1 mark

2 Why were the villagers unable to catch the bird?

....

☐ 1 mark

3 Where did the villagers store their food?

....

☐ 2 marks

Challenge 3

1 Why do you think the villagers were storing food for the winter?

....

....

☐ 1 mark

2 Why are the villagers unable to see the bird when it is in the yellowwood tree?

....

☐ 1 mark

3 Do you think the villagers saw the bird stealing food and animals from the fields at night? Give a reason for your answer.

....

☐ 2 marks

Total: _____ / 12 marks

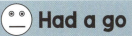 **Had a go** ☐   **Getting there** ☐   **Got it!** ☐

A Dragonfly

When the heat of the summer
Made drowsy the land,
A dragonfly came
And sat on my hand.

With its blue jointed body,
And wings like spun glass,
It lit on my fingers
As though they were grass.

by Eleanor Farjeon

Challenge 1

1 What colour is the dragonfly's body? ....

1 mark

2 'Made drowsy the land…' Circle the word below that is
   closest in meaning to 'drowsy'.

   sick   bright   warm   sleepy

1 mark

3 In which season is the poem set? ....

1 mark

Challenge 2

1 Find and copy two groups of words that tell you that the dragonfly landed on the narrator's hand.

....

....

2 marks

2 Find and copy the simile that tells you that the dragonfly's wings were transparent (see-through).

....

1 mark

3 According to the poem, where might dragonflies usually sit?

....

1 mark

Challenge 3

1 Why do you think the dragonfly landed on the narrator's hand? Give two reasons.

....

....

2 marks

2 Find and copy the line that tells you that the whole of the countryside is affected by the heat.

....

1 mark

3 What do you think is the narrator's opinion of the dragonfly?

....

1 mark

Total: _____ / 11 marks

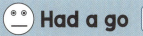 **Had a go** **Getting there** **Got it!**

A Book of Bears

BROWN BEARS

Ursus arctos

There are about 200,000 brown bears living across the world. They are widespread, with populations in North America, northern Europe, and northern Asia.

There are around 15 different subspecies* of brown bear. They vary in size and their colors range from very light brown to almost black. Here are a few of them.

Mainland* Grizzly Bear

Ursus arctos horribilis

The word grizzly means "tipped with gray." These bears get their name from the gray specks found all over their fur. They live in North America.

Syrian Brown Bear

Ursus arctos syriacus

These bears tend to be quite light in color and they are one of the smaller brown bear subspecies. They live in the Middle East.

Kodiak Bear

Ursus arctos middendorffi

These are the largest of the brown bears. They live on Kodiak Island in Alaska and are sometimes called the Alaskan brown bear.

by Katie Viggers

* subspecies: a subgroup within a species that has different traits to the main species

* mainland: the main part of a country

Challenge 1

1. What colour are the specks in a grizzly bear's fur? ....

   1 mark

2. Find and copy the words that tell you that different types of brown bears are different sizes.

   ....

   1 mark

3 Using information from the text, tick one box in each row to show whether each statement is **true** or **false**.

		True	False
a)	Brown bears can be found in northern Europe.		
b)	Brown bears are sometimes white.		
c)	Kodiak bears are also known as Syrian brown bears.		
d)	Grizzly bears get their name from the sound they make.		

4 marks

Challenge 2

1 What is the name of the largest type of brown bear?

....

1 mark

2 Where do Syrian brown bears live? ....

1 mark

3 How many subspecies of brown bear are there? ....

1 mark

Challenge 3

1 Identify a bear known by two different names and give both its names.

....

2 marks

2 Do you think all Syrian brown bears look the same? Give a reason for your answer.

....

....

2 marks

3 'There are about 200,000 brown bears living across the world.' Why do you think it is not possible to say exactly how many brown bears there are?

....

1 mark

Total: _____ / 14 marks

😐 **Had a go** ☐   🙂 **Getting there** ☐   😃 **Got it!** ☐

The Sheep-Pig

'What's that noise?' said Mrs Hogget, sticking her comfortable round red face out of the kitchen window. 'Listen, there 'tis again, did you hear it, what a racket, what a row, anybody'd think someone was being murdered, oh dearie me, whatever is it, just listen to it, will you?'

Farmer Hogget listened. From the usually quiet valley below the farm came a medley of sounds: the oompah oompah of a brass band, the shouts of children, the rattle and thump of a skittle alley, and every now and then a very high, very loud, very angry-sounding squealing lasting perhaps ten seconds.

Farmer Hogget pulled out an old pocket-watch as big round as a saucer and looked at it. 'Fair starts at two,' he said. 'It's started.'

'I knows that,' said Mrs Hogget, 'because I'm late now with all theseyer cakes and jams and pickles and preserves as is meant to be on the Produce Stall this very minute, and who's going to take them there, I'd like to know, why you are, but afore you does, what's that noise?'

The squealing sounded again.

'That noise?'

Mrs Hogget nodded a great many times. Everything that she did was done at great length, whether it was speaking or simply nodding her head. Farmer Hogget, on the other hand, never wasted his energy or his words.

'Pig,' he said.

by Dick King-Smith

Challenge 1

1. 'From the usually quiet valley below the farm came a medley of sounds…' Circle the word below that is similar in meaning to 'medley'.

   rumble   **rush**   **mixture**   **whisper**

   1 mark

2. What time did the fair start? ....

   1 mark

3 Using information from the text, tick one box in each row to show whether each statement is true or false.

	True	False
a) Mrs Hogget is in the kitchen.		
b) The sounds are coming from a circus.		
c) Mrs Hogget has a round red face.		
d) Mr Hogget's watch is very large.		

4 marks

Challenge 2

1 Find and copy two things Mrs Hogget is sending to the Produce Stall at the fair. ....

2 marks

2 Name two things that Mr Hogget does not waste.

....

2 marks

3 Find and copy the phrase that suggests that the farm is on a hill.

....

1 mark

Challenge 3

1 Find two pieces of evidence that suggest that Mrs Hogget does not like the sound she hears at the start of the extract.

....

....

2 marks

2 What evidence is there in the text to suggest that fairs do not happen very often in the valley?

....

1 mark

3 Why do you think the children are shouting?

....

1 mark

Total: _____ / 15 marks

😐 **Had a go** ☐   🙂 **Getting there** ☐   😄 **Got it!** ☐

21

The Magnificent Bull

My bull is white like the silver fish in the river,

White like the shimmering crane bird on the river bank,

White like fresh milk!

His roar is like thunder to the Turkish cannon on the steep shore.

My bull is dark like the raincloud in the storm.

He is like summer and winter.

Half of him is dark like the storm cloud

Half of him is light like sunshine.

His back shines like the morning star.

His brow is red like the back of the hornbill.

His forehead is like a flag, calling the people from a distance.

He resembles the rainbow.

I will water him at the river,

With my spear I shall drive my enemies.

Let them water their herds at the well;

The river belongs to me and my bull.

Drink, my bull, from the river; I am here

to guard you with my spear.

by Fiona Waters (from Dinka poem, translator unknown)

Challenge 1

1 The title of the poem is 'The Magnificent Bull'. Circle the word below that is closest in meaning to 'magnificent'.

huge	splendid	fierce	famous

1 mark

2 What colour are the fish in the river? ....

1 mark

3 '…the shimmering crane bird on the river bank…' Circle the word below that is similar in meaning to 'shimmering'.

gleaming   shaking   feathered   tall

1 mark

Challenge 2

1 Find and copy two colours that are used to describe the bull.

2 marks

2 Write down two places the people take their animals to drink.

2 marks

3 The narrator compares the bull to the weather in the first verse. Find another example at the end of the first verse where this is also done.

1 mark

Challenge 3

1 What do you think the narrator's opinion of the bull is? Give a reason for your answer.

2 marks

2 Why do you think the narrator says: 'He is like summer and winter'?

1 mark

3 Why do you think the narrator wants the bull to drink at the river?

1 mark

Total: _____ / 12 marks

😐 Had a go ☐   🙂 Getting there ☐   😄 Got it! ☐

Who Are You Calling Weird?

Aye-Aye

Nighttime. We are deep in a rainforest. Listen. Do you hear that tap-tapping? No, it isn't a woodpecker knocking on a tree with its beak. It's something much stranger. It's an aye-aye, rapping on a branch with its long, skeletal finger.

Because of its floppy, leathery ears and continuously-growing sharp teeth, people once thought the aye-aye was a rodent. But it's actually a lemur, a type of primate found only on Madagascar. Most lemurs are active during the day, but the aye-aye is nocturnal. Its huge eyes can see well even in low light and, unlike all other lemurs, it has that special middle finger which it taps on trees. It is listening for the echo that says there's a hollow tunnel beneath the bark. Inside the tunnel are tasty insect larvae. With sharp nails, the aye-aye tears open the bark and uses its fingers to fish out its meal.

Aye-ayes can live in other environments besides forests. They often venture into farms and villages, where they feast on coconuts and other fruits. This makes them unpopular with farmers. Some people don't just dislike aye-ayes; they fear them. They believe that if an aye-aye points its finger at you, then you will die. So they think that aye-ayes should be killed before they can do harm. The truth is that humans are more of a threat to aye-ayes than vice versa. The only critters that should fear these gentle lemurs are bugs!

by Marilyn Singer

Challenge 1

1 '…rapping on a branch…' Circle the word below that is closest in meaning to 'rapping'.

hugging   **pointing**   **knocking**   **touching**

1 mark

2 Find and copy the adjective that tells you that the aye-aye's finger is bony.

....

☐ I mark

3 Which country do aye-ayes come from? ....

☐ I mark

Challenge 2

I Find two ways the aye-aye is different from other lemurs.

....

☐ 2 marks

2 Other than insect larvae, which two foods do aye-ayes eat?

....

☐ 2 marks

3 How do the aye-aye's large eyes help it?

....

☐ I mark

Challenge 3

I Why do you think aye-ayes venture into farms and villages?

....

☐ I mark

2 According to the text, should humans be afraid of aye-ayes?
Give a reason for your answer.

....

☐ 2 marks

3 Write another word that is similar in meaning to 'critters' in the final
sentence of the extract.

....

☐ I mark

Total: _____ / 12 marks

 Had a go ☐   **Getting there** ☐   😄 **Got it!** ☐

Bill's New Frock

When Bill Simpson woke up on Monday morning, he found he was a girl.

He was still standing staring at himself in the mirror, quite baffled, when his mother swept in.

'Why don't you wear this pretty pink dress?' she said.

'I *never* wear dresses,' Bill burst out.

'I know,' his mother said. 'It's such a pity.'

And, to his astonishment, before he could even begin to argue, she had dropped the dress over his head and zipped up the back.

'I'll leave you to do up the shell buttons,' she said. 'They're a bit fiddly and I'm late for work.'

And she swept out, leaving him staring in dismay at the mirror. In it, a girl with his curly red hair and wearing a pretty pink frock with fiddly shell buttons was staring back at him in equal dismay.

'This can't be true,' Bill Simpson said to himself. 'This cannot be true!'

He stepped out of his bedroom just as his father was rushing past. He, too, was late in getting off to work.

Mr Simpson leaned over and planted a kiss on Bill's cheek.

'Bye, Poppet,' he said, ruffling Bill's curls. 'You look very sweet today. It's not often we see you in a frock, is it?'

He ran down the stairs and out of the house so quickly he didn't see Bill's scowl, or hear what he muttered savagely under his breath.

by Anne Fine

Challenge 1

1 '…staring in dismay in the mirror.' Circle the word below that is closest in meaning to 'dismay'.

alarm   **disgust**   **joy**   **excitement**

☐ I mark

2 Find and copy a word with a similar meaning to 'dress'. ....

☐ I mark

3 What colour is Bill's hair? ....

☐ I mark

26

Challenge 2

1 Give two reasons why the word 'never' is in italics.

....

....

2 marks

2 Why do you think Bill keeps staring in the mirror?

....

1 mark

3 '…his mother swept in.'

a) What does the word 'swept' suggest about the way Bill's mother was moving? ....

1 mark

b) Why do you think she is moving like this?

....

1 mark

Challenge 3

1 Do you think Bill's parents were surprised he was a girl? Give a reason for your answer.

....

2 marks

2 At the start of the extract, Bill feels 'baffled'. How have his feelings changed by the end of the extract?

....

1 mark

3 What do you think might happen next in the story? Explain your prediction.

....

....

2 marks

Total: _____ / 13 marks

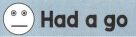 **Had a go**   **Getting there**   **Got it!**

Making Mistakes

Everybody makes mistakes,

That much I can confirm.

You can view them as a problem,

Or instead, a chance to learn.

For every great success that comes,

Is built upon the rubble,

Of accidents and failed attempts,

And countless hours of trouble.

But what you take from each mistake,

Remains inside your brain.

So when you start things over,

You won't make that one again.

by Daniel Thompson

Challenge 1

1 'That much I can confirm.' Circle the word below that is most similar in meaning to 'confirm'.

verify   deny   imagine   guess

1 mark

2 Who does the narrator say makes mistakes? ....

1 mark

3 Write another word that is similar in meaning to 'rubble'.

....

1 mark

Challenge 2

1 Does the narrator suggest it is possible to be successful without making a mistake? Give a reason for your answer.

....

....

2 marks

2 Find and copy the phrase that tells you that people have to spend a lot of time making mistakes before they can be successful.

....

1 mark

3 Why does the narrator say you will not make the same mistake again?

....

1 mark

Challenge 3

1 Summarise what the narrator is saying about making mistakes.

....

....

2 marks

Total: _____ / 9 marks

😐 **Had a go** ☐   🙂 **Getting there** ☐   😀 **Got it!** ☐

29

The Magic and Mystery of Trees

Temperate rainforests

Thick, lush rainforests grow in the world's wettest places. That means **lots of rain!** Unlike tropical forests, temperate rainforests grow in areas of **mild weather**, where it neither gets too hot nor too cold. Many of the trees are conifers.

Feel of the forest

The world's largest temperate rainforest grows along the west coast of North America. It is made up mostly of **conifers**, including the tallest trees in the world, giant redwoods. The trees grow so well because they have plenty of water. The rain is heaviest in winter but the summer months bring **thick, damp fogs** rolling off the oceans.

River beavers

Beavers build **dams** across forest streams. They gnaw through **saplings** (young trees) with their sharp front teeth. **Timber!** The tree crashes down to become part of the dam.

Big cats

Pumas are large cats that silently slink through the forest. They **pounce** on animals as large as deer, and kill them by biting on their necks.

Tree frogs

Pacific tree frogs live in forest **ponds** and damp ditches. They are brown, grey or green, but can **change colour** to blend in with their surroundings.

Raccoons

These scrappy mammals have a broad black stripe across their eyes, like a **bandit's mask**. They act like bandits too, raiding birds' nests to steal eggs.

Gentle giants

Elk are a type of very large deer. Males have **impressive antlers**. Elk glide among the trees, munching ferns, grass, twigs, and tree bark.

Cheeky chipmunks

Chipmunks are nimble little rodents that scamper through the forest searching for nuts, fruits and seeds. They carry food back to their burrow in their bulging **cheek pouches**.

by Jen Green

Challenge 1

1 According to the text, what is the world's tallest tree?

....

1 mark

2 The text is about temperate rainforests. What is the other type of forest it mentions? ....

....

1 mark

3 Where is the world's largest temperate rainforest?

....

1 mark

Challenge 2

1 Find two words used by the writer to describe the size of elk.

....

2 marks

2 What does the word 'glide' tell you about how elk move?

....

1 mark

3 '…nimble little rodents…' Circle the word below that is closest in meaning to 'nimble'.

cute   **alert**   **agile**   **furry**

1 mark

Challenge 3

1 Do you think it would be easy to see a tree frog? Give a reason for your answer. ....

....

2 marks

2 Why do you think it might be useful for a puma to move 'silently'?

....

1 mark

3 Which of the animals in the text would you most like to see? Give a reason for your answer. ....

2 marks

Total: _____ / 12 marks

😐 **Had a go** ☐   🙂 **Getting there** ☐   😃 **Got it!** ☐

31

The Boy at the Back of the Class by Onjali Rauf

I'm lucky because Tom and Josie and Michael always help me with the things I get stuck with. They're my best friends and we do everything together.

Tom's got short spiky hair and a side-smile and a big Adam's apple that looks like a ping-pong ball got stuck in his throat. He's the smallest in our group but he's also the funniest. He only joined our class last year after his parents moved here from America, but we became friends instantly. He has three older brothers who all tease and bully him. Not seriously – only for a joke. But I think they steal his food too which is why he's so skinny and always super-hungry. I once saw him eat a whole pizza with extra toppings and a double cheeseburger for lunch and still not be full up! So I hide my snacks and chocolate bars from him when I can.

Josie has large, brown eyes and at least a million freckles across her face. She's tall and gangly and is always chewing on her hair. She's the fastest girl in our year and can kick a football past any goalie from the other side of the pitch. She's the coolest person I know, and I've known her since we were three. Our mums say we became instant friends the first day we started nursery, so they decided to become friends too. I don't really remember much about myself at that age, but Josie is in all my school memories. We even got our first detention together last year – all because of a hamster called Herbert.

1. **Reorganise the phrases to create the definition of what a narrator is. Write the sentence.**

    who tells   the story.   the character   The narrator is

    ....

    1 mark

2. **Do you think the narrator of this story is a child or an adult? Give a reason for your answer.**

    ....

    ....

    2 marks

3. **What is an adjective?**

....

1 mark

4. **Find and copy two adjectives used to compare Tom with the other children.**

....

2 marks

5. **Which of the narrator's friends is not described in the extract?**

....

1 mark

6. **Write down one thing the narrator admires about each of his/her friends.**

Tom	
Josie	

2 marks

7. **Why do you think the narrator hides his/her snacks and chocolate bars from Tom?**

....

1 mark

8. **Do you think Josie really has 'at least a million freckles'? Give a reason for your answer.**

....

2 marks

The Ghost Teacher by Allan Ahlberg

The school is closed, the children gone,
But the ghost of a teacher lingers on.
As the daylight fades, as the daytime ends,
As the night draws in and the dark descends,
She stands in the classroom, as clear as glass,
And calls the names of her absent class.

The school is shut, the children grown,
But the ghost of the teacher, all alone,
Puts the date on the board and moves about
(As the night draws on and the stars come out)
Between the desks – a glow in the gloom –
And calls for quiet in the silent room.

The school is a ruin, the children fled,
But the ghost of the teacher, long-time dead,
As the moon comes up and the first owls glide,
Puts on her coat and steps outside.
In the moonlit playground, shadow-free,
She stands on duty with a cup of tea.

The school is forgotten – children forget –
But the ghost of a teacher lingers yet.
As the night creeps up to the edge of the day,
She tidies the Plasticine away;
Counts the scissors – a shimmer of glass –
And says, 'Off you go!' to her absent class.

She utters the words that no one hears,

Picks up her bag …

        and

                disappears.

9. '...as clear as glass...' Find and copy another phrase that tells you that the teacher is transparent like glass.

....

10. '...a teacher lingers yet.' Circle the word below that is closest in meaning to 'lingers'.

        waits   remains   shimmers   watches

11. Using information from the text, tick one box in each row to show whether each statement is true or false.

	True	False
a) There are children in the school.		
b) The poem takes place during the daytime.		
c) The Ghost Teacher has no shadow.		
d) It is quiet inside the school.		

12. How long do you think the school has been closed for? Give a reason for your answer.

....

13. Find and copy two phrases from different parts of the poem that show how time is passing during the night.

....

....

14. Why do you think the teacher disappears at the end of the poem?

....

....

Total: _____ / 23 marks

The Magic Finger

The farm next to ours is owned by Mr and Mrs Gregg. The Greggs have two children, both of them boys. Their names are Philip and William. Sometimes I go over to their farm to play with them.

I am a girl and I am eight years old.

Philip is also eight years old.

William is three years older. He is ten.

What?

Oh, all right then.

He is eleven.

Last week, something very funny happened to the Gregg family. I am going to tell you about it as best I can.

Now the one thing that Mr Gregg and his two boys loved to do more than anything else was to go hunting. Every Sunday morning they would take their guns and go off into the woods to look for animals and birds to shoot. Even Philip, who was only eight years old, had a gun of his own.

I can't stand hunting. I just can't *stand* it. It doesn't seem right to me that men and boys should kill animals just for the fun they get out of it. So I used to try to stop Philip and William from doing it. Every time I went over to their farm I would do my best to talk them out of it, but they only laughed at me.

I even said something about it once to Mr Gregg, but he just walked on past me as if I wasn't there.

Then, one Saturday morning, I saw Philip and William coming out of the woods with their father, and they were carrying a lovely young deer.

This made me so cross that I started shouting at them.

The boys laughed and made faces at me, and Mr Gregg told me to go home and mind my own P's and Q's.

Well, that did it!

I saw red.

And before I was able to stop myself, I did something I never meant to do.
I PUT THE MAGIC FINGER ON THEM ALL!

by Roald Dahl

Challenge 1

1 Choose the correct word to complete the sentence.

The narrator of the story cannot .... hunting.

      go   **like**   **bear**   **hate**

1 mark

2 How old is the oldest child in the text? Circle your answer.

     eight years old   **ten years old**

     eleven years old   **twelve years old**

1 mark

3 Using information from the text, tick one box in each row to show whether each statement is true or false.

	True	False
a) Philip owns a gun.		
b) Birds and animals live in the woods.		
c) The narrator goes hunting with the Gregg family.		
d) William and Philip agree with the narrator's views about hunting.		

4 marks

Challenge 2

1 Find and copy the words that tell you that the narrator lives on a farm.

....

1 mark

2 'Sometimes I go over to their farm to play with them.' Find another place in the text where the narrator tells us she goes to the farm. Copy the phrase.

....

1 mark

3 What do you think has happened to the young deer? Give a reason for your answer.

....

....

....

....

2 marks

4 'I PUT THE MAGIC FINGER ON THEM ALL!' Why has the writer used capital letters for this sentence?

....

1 mark

Challenge 3

1 '…he just walked on past me as if I wasn't there.' What does this phrase suggest about how Mr Gregg feels about the narrator?

....

....

2 marks

2 What evidence is there that the Gregg family go to woods to shoot animals? Find two examples.

....

....

....

....

2 marks

3 What do you think will happen next in the story?

....

....

1 mark

Total: _____ / 16 marks

 Had a go ☐   **Getting there** ☐   **Got it!** ☐

GRRRR

If you smile then I will glare,
If you're sad then I don't care,
If you tell me I've been bad, I will say 'Oh
    good, I'm glad!'

I don't want to, I don't like you!
If you touch me, I will bite you!

If you try to calm me down, I will roll round
    on the ground.
If you try to make me stop, I will scream until
    I pop.
If you shh me, I will yell and yeLL and yELL
    and YELL and YELL!

I don't want to, I don't like you!
If you touch me, I will bite you!

If you try to make me eat, I'll spit my food out
    on the floor,
If you try to make me sleep, I'll bang my head
    against the door.
If you sing a lullaby, I'll join in the key of Y!

I don't want to, I don't like you!
If you touch me, I will bite you!

I'm the worst there's ever been, I'm the worst
    you've ever seen,
I'm a single-handed RIOT!!!!!!!!!!!!!!!!!!!!!!!!!!!
    !!

(Now I'm ready to be quiet)

by Francesca Beard

Challenge 1

1 Which of these words is closest in meaning to 'glare', as it is used in the poem?

       glow   **grin**   **scowl**   **scream**

1 mark

2 Choose the correct word to complete the sentence:

If the narrator were told they were bad, they say they would

feel ....

       angry   **pleased**   **grateful**   **amused**

1 mark

3 'I don't want to…' List three things the narrator says they don't want to do.

3 marks

4 Find two words that rhyme with 'sad'.

2 marks

Challenge 2

1 Which line suggests the narrator does not care about how their behaviour makes other people feel?

1 mark

2 'If you sing a lullaby…' Why might someone sing a lullaby to the narrator?

1 mark

3 'I will yell and yeLL and yELL
    and YELL and YELL!'

Why has the poet used capital letters in this way?

1 mark

4 Why has the writer used so many exclamation marks towards the end of the poem?

1 mark

40

Challenge 3

1 Do you think the narrator would really bite someone if they touched them? Give a reason for your answer.

....

....

2 '…single-handed RIOT' What does this phrase, and the use of capital letters, suggest about the behaviour of the narrator?

....

....

3 How does the narrator feel by the end of the poem?

....

....

Total: _____ / 16 marks

😐 Had a go ☐   🙂 Getting there ☐   😃 Got it! ☐

Africa, Amazing Africa: Country by Country

The first human beings to walk this planet were Africans. Some made a long journey out of Africa and ended up populating the rest of the world. So we are all from Africa – if you go back far enough.

Africa is *amazing*. It is a gigantic continent: as big as Europe, the USA and Mexico, India and Japan all put together! At the moment, it is divided into 55 countries – and each of those countries has an incredible history and geography, and its own culture, languages and biodiversity.

Africa is hot, blinding deserts; wild, wet deltas; dark, dripping rainforests; white, sandy beaches; flat, grassy savannahs; cold, snowy mountains; black-volcano islands; deep blue oceans and more...

Africa is modern mega-cities with skyscrapers and motorways. Africa is ancient cities of clay with mosques and libraries. Africa is villages of huts with goats and chickens. Africa is shanty-towns made out of cardboard and corrugated iron.

Africa is donkeys and diamonds, camels and Coca-Cola, Lamborghinis and lions, oil-rigs and armies, football and voodoo, and more...

Africa is people – billions of people. Light people and dark people, tall people and short people, plump people and skinny people. People playing music, playing football, playing board games and computer games. People dancing, texting, coding and studying studying studying. People in offices, in traffic, in queues. People selling food and water and mobile phones. People shouting and singing and smiling. And almost half the people on the African continent are young people – we are the youngest population on the planet!

by Atinuke

Challenge 1

1. 'Africa is *amazing*. It is a gigantic continent…' Write down a word that is similar in meaning to 'gigantic'. _____

1 mark

2. Write down the adjective used to describe the history and geography of African countries.

....

1 mark

3. Non-fiction texts often contain statistics (numbers). Find one statistic about Africa in the text.

....

1 mark

4. The text mentions modern and ancient cities. Name two other types of settlements where people in Africa live.

....

2 marks

Challenge 2

1. 'Africa is *amazing*.' Why do you think the writer chose to put the word 'amazing' in italics?

....

1 mark

2. 'It is a gigantic continent: as big as Europe, the USA and Mexico, India and Japan all put together!' Why do you think the writer has used an exclamation mark at the end of this sentence?

....

....

1 mark

3. '…studying studying studying.' Why do you think the writer has repeated the word 'studying'?

....

1 mark

4 Find and copy two phrases that show contrasting temperatures in Africa.

....

....

2 marks

5 'donkeys and diamonds' is an example of alliteration because both words start with the same sound. Can you find another example?

....

1 mark

Challenge 3

1 Do you think the text is really saying that each of us comes from Africa? Give a reason for your answer.

....

....

2 marks

2 'At the moment, it is divided into 55 countries...' What does the phrase 'At the moment' suggest about how Africa might change over time?

....

1 mark

3 Has anything you have read about Africa surprised you?

....

....

1 mark

4 '...dark, dripping rainforests...' Why might a rainforest be 'dark'?

....

1 mark

Total: _____ / 16 marks

 Had a go ☐   **Getting there** ☐   😀 **Got it!** ☐

44

Mr Majeika

It was Monday morning, it was pouring with rain, and it was everyone's first day back at St Barty's Primary School after the Christmas holidays. That's why Class Three were in a bad temper.

Pandora Green had been rude to Melanie, so Melanie was crying (though Melanie always found *something* to cry about). Hamish Bigmore was trying to pick a quarrel with Thomas and Pete, the twins. And Mr Potter the head teacher was very cross because the new teacher for Class Three hadn't turned up.

'I can't think where he is,' he grumbled at Class Three. 'He should have been here at nine o'clock for the beginning of school. And now it's nearly ten, and I should be teaching Class Two. We'll have to open the folding doors and let you share the lesson with them.'

Class Three groaned. They thought themselves very important people, and didn't in the least want to share a lesson with Class Two, who were just babies.

'Bother this thing,' muttered Mr Potter, struggling with the folding doors that separated the classrooms.

'*I'll* help you, Mr Potter,' said Hamish Bigmore, who didn't really want to help at all, but just to be a nuisance as usual. And then everyone else began to shout: 'Don't let Hamish Bigmore do it, he's no good, let *me* help,' so that in a moment there was uproar.

But suddenly silence fell. And there was a gasp.

Mr Potter was still fiddling with the folding doors, so he didn't see what was happening. But Class Three did.

One of the big windows in the classroom slid open all by itself, and *something* flew in.

It was a man on a magic carpet.

There could be no doubt about that. Class Three knew a magic carpet when they saw one. After all, they'd read *Aladdin* and all that sort of stuff. There are magic carpets all over the place in *Aladdin*. But this wasn't *Aladdin*. This was St Barty's Primary School on a wet Monday morning. And magic carpets don't turn up in schools. Class Three knew that. So they stared.

by Humphrey Carpenter

Challenge 1

1 In what season does the story take place?

....

1 mark

2 What are the names of the twins in the story?

....

1 mark

3 'Hamish Bigmore was trying to pick a quarrel...' Circle the word below that is closest in meaning to 'quarrel.'

debate   **argument**   **question**   **friendship**

1 mark

4 '...there was uproar.' Circle the word below that is closest in meaning to 'uproar'.

outrage   **commotion**   **humour**   **silence**

1 mark

Challenge 2

1 'Melanie always found *something* to cry about' Why do you think the writer used italics for the word 'something'?

....

1 mark

2 Do you think the children in Class Three like wet weather? Give a reason for your answer.

....

....

2 marks

3 Find two words from different parts of the text that describe how Mr Potter speaks and that show he is very cross.

....

2 marks

4 How do the children in Class Three show they do not want to share their lesson with Class Two? ....

1 mark

5 On a normal day, would the sliding doors be open or closed? Give a reason for your answer.

....

2 marks

Challenge 3

1 How would you describe the character Hamish Bigmore? Give reasons from the text to support your ideas.

....

....

2 marks

2 'But suddenly silence fell. And there was a gasp.' Why do you think the children gasp at this point in the story? Give a reason for your answer.

....

....

2 marks

3 What does the window sliding open by itself suggest about what might happen next?

....

....

1 mark

4 What evidence is there in the text to suggest that *Aladdin* is not the only book the children have read in which there are magic carpets?

....

1 mark

Total: _____ / 18 marks

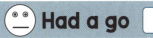 **Had a go** ☐   **Getting there** ☐  **Got it!** ☐

The Princess's Treasures

The Princess owned a whole turret of
    treasures.

There was a toy dragon that breathed
    real sparks,
A necklace made from the stony tears
    of statues,
A wooden unicorn that danced on a
    lawn of green glass,
A casket of blue shells from a
    mermaid's cave
And a tiny spinning wheel
That could turn spider silk into birdsong.

Yet the thing she loved the best
Was a scruffy crimson rug.

Its patterns had been stolen by the
    desert sun,
Its fringes had been frayed by ice
    storms,
Its tufts had been flattened by sleeping
    tigers,
But still it rippled across her room
Like an ancient flying fish,
And when it slept beside her bed
It smelled of spices
And meadow flowers
And salty seas.

by Clare Bevan

Challenge 1

1 'A casket of blue shells…' Write another word that is similar in meaning to 'casket'.

_____

2 '…a scruffy crimson rug.' Circle the word below that is closest in meaning to 'scruffy'.

      scorched   **dirty**   **shabby**   **short**

3 What colour is 'crimson'? Circle your answer.

      brown   **blue**   **red**   **green**

4 Find and copy three examples of mythical creatures mentioned in the poem.

_____

5 Copy the adjective that tells you that the rug is old.

_____

Challenge 2

1 What does the word 'turret' suggest about where the princess lives?

_____

2 Do you think the princess's necklace could really exist? Give a reason for your answer.

_____

_____

3 Find two pieces of evidence from the text that support the idea that the rug is 'scruffy'.

_____

4 Copy the words that tell you that the colours on the rug have faded.

....

1 mark

5 'But still it rippled across her room...' What does the word 'rippled' suggest about the way the rug moves?

....

1 mark

Challenge 3

1 Why do you think somebody might want a spinning wheel that turns spider silk into birdsong?

....

1 mark

2 Find two pieces of evidence from the poem that suggest that the rug has been to many different places.

....

....

2 marks

3 What do you think the rug really is? Give a reason for your answer.

....

....

2 marks

4 Which of the princess's treasures would you most like to own? Give a reason for your answer.

....

....

2 marks

Total: _____ / 21 marks

 Had a go ☐   **Getting there** ☐   😃 **Got it!** ☐

50

Recipe for Fire

Sit up and pay attention, it's time for a science lesson! When you think about it, a chemical experiment is like a recipe – you take the ingredients and make something new. And this is what we need to make fire. This particular recipe is a chemistry recipe, because that's what fire actually is – one of the products of a chemical reaction. Fire has three basic ingredients: fuel, oxygen and heat. You need all three ingredients in the recipe to make fire start. Luckily, if you understand how to make fire, you will also have a good idea of how to stop it!

Ingredients for fire

1. Oxygen: this is easy enough to source, as nature provides it! There's oxygen in the air we breathe.
2. Fuel: you could use a number of different fuel sources, but let's stick to the fuel our ancestors first used, wood.
3. Kindling: this is a dried out version of our fuel, with a low water content, so it burns more easily and will get the fire going.
4. A spark: you need this to set the fire off in the first place.
5. Combustion: this is the chemical reaction needed to keep the fire going.

1. PREPARE THE SITE

Pick a site for your fire and a material you can use as fuel. We've chosen wood for our recipe, but nature uses anything that will actually burn, and which contains carbon.

2. LAY THE KINDLING

Kindling is the material used for lighting fires. It is often a very dry version of the main fuel and burns easily which creates the perfect conditions for the main source of fuel to ignite and keep burning.

3. IGNITE THE SPARK

A spark is a hot, glowing particle that gets a fire going. The spark provides the heat to combine the chemicals in the fuel with the oxygen in the air. Sparks can be made by nature, such as volcanoes or lightning, or by rubbing sticks together to create friction. Today, people also use matches – but don't do this unless an adult is present!

4. COMBUSTION

This is the reaction between the fuel and the oxygen in the air, which allows the fire to flame. Beware – if you remove either the fuel, the oxygen or the combustion (i.e. the heat), the fire will stop. **by Mark Brake**

Challenge 1

1 Name one of the three basic ingredients you need to make fire.

....

2 What kind of reaction makes fire?

....

3 'IGNITE THE SPARK' Circle the word below that is closest in meaning to the word 'ignite' in this heading.

burn　　　**set**　　　**light**　　　**heat**

4 '...this is easy enough to source...' Write down another word with a similar meaning to 'source' as it is used in this sentence.

....

Challenge 2

1 What was the first fuel used by humans to make fire?

....

2 Can you make a fire without fuel? Support your answer with evidence from the text.

....

....

3 Why should you not use matches without an adult present?

....

4 Why might you need to know how to stop fire?

....

5 According to the text, how does kindling compare to wood?

....

Challenge 3

1 Do you think something with a high water content would burn well? Support your answer with evidence from the text.

....

....

2 marks

2 Which section gives you information about how to put out a fire?

....

1 mark

3 'Pick a site for your fire...' Why do you think people need to think carefully about where they start a fire?

....

1 mark

4 Why do you think people prefer to use matches to start fires today?

....

1 mark

5 Describe how a fire could happen naturally. Make sure you include the three ingredients, fuel, oxygen and heat, in your description.

....

....

....

....

....

3 marks

Total: _____ / 18 marks

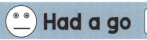 Had a go ☐   Getting there ☐   Got it! ☐

Tree by James Carter

A tree

is not like you and

me – it waits around quite

patiently – catching kites and

dropping leaves – reaching out to touch

the breeze…A tree all day will stand and stare

clothed in summer, winter : bare – it has no shame

or modesty…Perhaps its generosity is the greatest in

the world – it gives a home to every bird, every squirrel,

feeds them too – to every dog it is a loo…And after dark

what does it do? Catch a falling star or two? Shimmy

in the old moonlight? Or maybe have a conker fight?

A tree can give an awful lot : the wood to make a

baby's cot – pencils, paper, tables, chairs – lolly

sticks as well as stairs…Without a tree we

could not live – a tree, it seems just

loves to give –

but us :

we

chop

we

take

we

burn

that's

what we

do in return

1. Name two animals for whom trees provide a home.

....

2. Name something else the narrator says you might find in a tree.

....

3. 'clothed in summer, winter : bare' What does this line of the poem mean?

....

....

4. Why does the narrator not know for sure what the tree does at night?

....

5. 'Shimmy in the old moonlight?' Why do you think the poet has used the adjective 'old' to describe the moonlight?

....

6. What do you think is the poet's opinion of trees?

....

7. Do you think the narrator thinks people treat trees fairly? Give a reason for your answer.

....

....

KAREN DARKE

British athlete and explorer

1971—present

By the time she was 21, Karen Darke had climbed both Mont Blanc and the Matterhorn mountains in the Alps, and had a promising adventuring career ahead of her. However, a trip to Scotland changed her life forever when she slipped off a cliff while rock climbing.

Karen's fall left her in a coma and with many injuries, including a broken skull, neck and back. When she eventually woke up, doctors told her she was paralysed from the chest down and would never walk again. This wasn't easy for Karen to accept and at first she felt very low. However, with time she realized that she was lucky to be alive. The first thing Karen bought when she got out of hospital was a racing wheelchair, and she has been unstoppable ever since.

Only one year after her accident, Karen put her new wheelchair to good use and took part in a half marathon, quickly followed by the London Marathon. Then, in 1997, Karen hand-cycled through the Himalayas, from Kazakhstan to Pakistan, making her the first woman paraplegic (person whose lower body and legs are paralysed) to do this. She went on to challenge herself in more and more extreme ways, from crossing Greenland on sit-skis, where Karen's paralysis made it tricky to know if she was getting too cold, to kayaking along the coast of Canada and Alaska for three months.

In 2010, Karen decided to become an athlete and joined the British para-cycling team. By 2016, she had entered the Paralympics twice, winning a silver medal in 2012, and gold in 2016! Karen Darke's abilities seem to know no limits.

8. Find two phrases from different parts of the text that suggest that Karen Darke will always be paralysed.

....

....

2 marks

9. '...she felt very low.' What do you think the writer means by this phrase? ....

1 mark

10. In which country did Karen Darke's 1997 trip end?

....

1 mark

11. Why do you think the writer explains what 'paraplegic' means?

....

....

1 mark

12. Give one reason why crossing Greenland was an 'extreme' challenge for Darke.

....

1 mark

13. What do you think is the writer's view of what Darke might achieve next? Give evidence from the text to support your answer.

....

....

2 marks

14. What do you think about Darke's achievements? Give a reason for your answer.

....

....

2 marks

Total: _____ / 19 marks

Stuart Little

The home of the Little family was a pleasant place near a park in New York City. In the mornings the sun streamed in through the east windows, and all the Littles were up early as a general rule. Stuart was a great help to his parents, and to his older brother George, because of his small size and because he could do things a mouse can do and was agreeable about doing them. One day when Mrs. Little was washing out the bathtub after Mr. Little had taken a bath, she lost a ring off her finger and was horrified to discover that it had fallen down the drain.

"What had I better do?" she cried, trying to keep the tears back.

"If I were you," said George, "I should bend a hairpin in the shape of a fishhook and tie it onto a piece of string and try to fish the ring out with it." So Mrs. Little found a piece of string and a hairpin, and for about a half-hour she fished for the ring; but it was dark down the drain and the hook always seemed to catch on something before she could get it down to where the ring was.

"What luck?" inquired Mr. Little, coming into the bathroom.

"No luck at all," said Mrs. Little. "The ring is so far down I can't fish it up."

"Why don't we send Stuart down after it?" suggested Mr. Little. "How about it, Stuart, would you like to try?"

"Yes, I would," Stuart replied, "but I think I'd better get into my old pants. I imagine it's wet down there."

"It's all of that," said George, who was a trifle annoyed that his hook idea hadn't worked.

So Stuart slipped into his old pants and prepared to go down the drain after the ring. He decided to carry the string along with him, leaving one end in charge of his father. "When I jerk three times on the string, pull me up," he said. And while Mr. Little knelt in the tub, Stuart slid easily down the drain and was lost to view. In a minute or so, there came three quick jerks on the string, and Mr. Little carefully hauled it up.

There, at the end, was Stuart, with the ring safely around his neck.

by E.B. White

Challenge 1

1 '...a pleasant place...' Circle the word below that is closest in meaning to 'pleasant'.

wealthy   sunny   agreeable   nearby

☐ 1 mark

2 Which of the brothers is younger, George or Stuart?

....

☐ 1 mark

3 '...was horrified to discover...' Circle the word below that is closest in meaning to 'horrified' in this sentence.

frightened   startled   shocked   sad

☐ 1 mark

4 What was near to the Little's home?

....

☐ 1 mark

5 '...when I jerk three times...' Circle the word below that is closest in meaning to 'jerk' in this sentence.

hang   fish   tremble   jolt

☐ 1 mark

Challenge 2

1 Do you think Stuart minded helping his family? Give a reason from the text to support your answer.

....

....

☐ 2 marks

2 Why might Mrs. Little have felt like crying when she lost her ring?

....

☐ 1 mark

3 Find three reasons why using the string and the hairpin to fish for the ring did not work.

....

....

☐ 3 marks

60

4 Why does Stuart change his clothes?

....

....

1 mark

Challenge 3

1 Do you think George is also small like a mouse? Give a reason for your answer.

....

....

2 marks

2 Why do you think George feels 'a trifle annoyed' when the hook idea doesn't work?

....

1 mark

3 What do you think it would have been like for Stuart down the drain? Give evidence from different parts of the text.

....

....

2 marks

4 How do you think Mrs Little would feel when she saw Stuart with the ring around his neck?

....

....

2 marks

Total: _____ / 19 marks

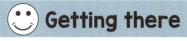 **Had a go**   **Getting there**   **Got it!**

Cinderella

I guess you think you know this story.
You don't. The real one's much more gory.
The phoney one, the one you know,
Was cooked up years and years ago,
And made to sound all soft and sappy
just to keep the children happy.
Mind you, they got the first bit right,
The bit where, in the dead of night,
The Ugly Sisters, jewels and all,
Departed for the Palace Ball,
While darling little Cinderella
Was locked up in a slimy cellar,
Where rats who wanted things to eat,
Began to nibble at her feet.

She bellowed 'Help!' and 'Let me out!'
The Magic Fairy heard her shout.
Appearing in a blaze of light,
She said: 'My dear, are you all right?'
'All right?' cried Cindy. 'Can't you see
'I feel as rotten as can be!'
She beat her fist against the wall,
And shouted, 'Get me to the Ball!
'There is a Disco at the Palace!
'The rest have gone and I am jealous!
'I want a dress! I want a coach!
'And earrings and a diamond brooch!
'And silver slippers, two of those!
'And lovely nylon panty hose!
'Done up like that I'll guarantee
'The handsome Prince will fall for me!'
The Fairy said, 'Hang on a tick.'
She gave her wand a mighty flick
And quickly, in no time at all,
Cindy was at the Palace Ball!

It made the Ugly Sisters wince
To see her dancing with the Prince.
She held him very tight and pressed
herself against his manly chest.
The Prince himself was turned to pulp,
All he could do was gasp and gulp.
Then midnight struck. She shouted, 'Heck!
I've got to run to save my neck!'
The Prince cried, 'No! Alas! Alack!'
He grabbed her dress to hold her back.
As Cindy shouted, 'Let me go!'
The dress was ripped from head to toe.

She ran out in her underwear,
And lost one slipper on the stair.
The Prince was on it like a dart,
He pressed it to his pounding heart,
'The girl this slipper fits,' he cried,
'Tomorrow morn shall be my bride!
'I'll visit every house in town
'Until I've tracked the maiden down!'
Then rather carelessly, I fear,
He placed it on a crate of beer.

by Roald Dahl

Challenge 1

1. 'The phoney one...' Circle the word below which is closest in meaning to the word 'phoney'.

   fake   **funny**   **scary**   **true**

   1 mark

2. What does the phrase 'in the dead of night' mean?

   ....

   1 mark

3. 'She bellowed "Help!" and "Let me out!"' In this line, what does the word 'bellowed' mean?

   ....

   1 mark

4. 'Done up like that I'll guarantee...' In this line, what does the word 'guarantee' mean?

   ....

   1 mark

5. 'Tomorrow morn shall be my bride!' In this line, what complete word is 'morn' short for?

   ....

   1 mark

Challenge 2

1. '...locked up in a slimy cellar...' How do you think the author wanted us to feel about Cinderella when he chose these words?

   ....

   1 mark

2. In the lines where Cinderella is shouting to the Magic Fairy, why do you think the author uses so many exclamation marks?

   ....

   1 mark

3. Which line in the poem tells us that the Magic Fairy did not take long to get Cinderella to the ball?

   ....

   1 mark

4. 'The Prince was on it like a dart...' Why does the poet use this simile to describe the Prince?

   ....

   1 mark

Challenge 3

1 At the start of the poem, why does the author suggest that the 'real' Cinderella story was rewritten into the one children will know?

....

☐ 1 mark

2 Why do you think Cinderella was 'locked up in a slimy cellar' by the Ugly Sisters?

....

....

☐ 2 marks

3 How did the Ugly Sisters feel when they saw Cinderella dancing with the Prince? Give evidence from the text to support your answer.

....

....

☐ 2 marks

4 'He pressed it to his pounding heart…' Why do you think the Prince's heart is 'pounding'?

....

☐ 1 mark

Total: _____ / 15 marks

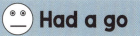

How to be a Scientist

MARY ANNING

Palaeontologist   Born in 1799   From the UK

Mary Anning came from a poor family. She figured out how to find amazing fossils, which are ancient animals or plants preserved in rock, and made money selling them. Some of her finds were 200 million years old, from the time of the dinosaurs! Now she is celebrated as a great fossil hunter who changed the way we see the world.

Fossil hunting

Anning made many important finds, including two ancient sea reptiles – the ichthyosaur and the plesiosaur. She also dug up amazing fossilized shells. People didn't believe there had been creatures living a long time ago that no longer existed, but Anning's discoveries proved otherwise.

No women allowed!

The Geological Society of London didn't allow Anning in because she was a woman. She also didn't always get credit for her findings. People today realise and appreciate just how important her discoveries really were.

Charles Darwin link

Geologist Adam Sedgwick bought many fossils from Anning. He taught geology to Charles Darwin at the University of Cambridge. Darwin may have been able to see and study some of Anning's fossils, helping him to develop his theory of evolution.

Lyme Regis

Most of Anning's fossil hunting took place where she lived – on the fossil-rich coast around Lyme Regis in the United Kingdom.

Coprolite

Anning's discoveries showed that a mysterious type of rock, now called coprolite, was actually fossilized poo.

Ichthyosaur

This sea reptile lived hundreds of millions of years ago. It had big eye sockets, probably so it could see well underwater.

Plesiosaur

The plesiosaur was the largest sea-dwelling reptile when it lived on Earth more than 205 million years ago.

Ammonite shell

This shell was Anning's most common find. It's the shell of a mollusc whose closest living relatives include the octopus, squid, and cuttlefish.

by Steve Mould

Challenge 1

1 Find an adjective from the first section that means 'very old'.

....

1 mark

2 Where was the Geological Society based?

....

1 mark

3 Where did Charles Darwin study?

....

1 mark

4 '...a mysterious type of rock...' Circle the word below that is closest in meaning to 'mysterious'.

strange   **fossilised**   **new**   **original**

1 mark

5 According to the text, how long ago did dinosaurs live?

....

1 mark

Challenge 2

1 What is another name given in the text for a fossil-hunter?

....

1 mark

2 '...fossil-rich coast...' What do you think 'fossil-rich' means?

....

1 mark

3 Write the name of an ancient creature that is related to animals living today, and the names of the related animals.

....

....

2 marks

4 Find an example of one way an ancient creature may have adapted to how it lived.

....

....

1 mark

5 How might Mary Anning's finds have helped her family?

....

☐ 1 mark

Challenge 3

1 Why did people not believe ancient animals used to exist before Anning made her discoveries?

....

....

☐ 1 mark

2 What evidence is there in the text that Adam Sedgwick valued Anning's work?

....

☐ 1 mark

3 'The Geological Society of London didn't allow Anning in because she was a woman.' What does this tell you about how women were treated at the time?

....

☐ 1 mark

4 How have people's opinions of Anning changed since she was alive?

....

....

☐ 1 mark

5 Can you think of a reason why it might have been helpful for the Ichthyosaur to be able to see well underwater?

....

☐ 1 mark

Total: _____ / 16 marks

 Had a go ☐   **Getting there** ☐   😃 **Got it!** ☐

Mindy Kim and the Yummy Seaweed Business

My name is Mindy Kim.

I'm seven and a half years old. That's old enough to ride a bike around our street, but not old enough to have my own puppy – or at least that's what my dad said.

I don't really agree with him, but our old apartment in California wasn't big enough for a puppy anyway. I looked it up, and the experts on the Internet say that puppies need lots of room to run outdoors.

Now that we've moved into a house with a big backyard, we can really get a puppy! I just have to convince my dad that it's a good idea first.

So far, no such luck. Dad wants me to prove that I can be "responsible" enough for a puppy first… and then he'll "consider" getting me one.

I decorated my own room to show Dad I'm "responsible". I'm trying to be more grown-up, so I only put three dog stuffed animals on my bed. There are ten more under my bed, but Dad doesn't need to know that. They'll just have to take turns.

After I finished, I was looking through a website on huskies, one of my *favorite* kinds of dogs, when I heard Dad say, "Mindy? Can you help me with these boxes?"

CRASH!

"Dad!" I ran downstairs to see him standing over a box of broken dishes.

"Oh no!" he said. "These were your mom's favorites."

He looked so sad, like he was about to cry. I wished I'd brought one of my stuffed dogs with me. I'd even let him hug Snowball, my favorite white husky.

I miss Mom, but I know Dad misses her a lot more. She died a few months ago because she was really sick for a long time.

"It's okay," I said. "It was an accident. Mom wouldn't be mad."

Dad smiled. "No, she wouldn't. She was nice like that."

Dad and I finished unpacking and cleaning up the kitchen. The kitchen in our apartment in California was way smaller, so our things only filled up half the cabinets in our new house.

by Lyla Lee

Challenge 1

1. Where has Mindy Kim moved from? .... ☐ 1 mark

2. '…convince my dad…' Write another word that is similar in meaning to 'convince'. .... ☐ 1 mark

3. How many stuffed dog toys does Mindy Kim own? .... ☐ 1 mark

4. According to the text, what is one thing puppies need?

   ....

   ☐ 1 mark

5. '…prove that I can be "responsible" enough…' Circle the word below that is closest in meaning to the word 'responsible' as it is used here.

   gentle   **sensible**   **calm**   **kind**

   ☐ 1 mark

Challenge 2

1. Name two things Mindy Kim researches on the internet.

   ....
   ....

   ☐ 2 marks

2. Find two pieces of evidence that support the idea that Mindy Kim likes huskies.

   ....
   ....
   ....

   ☐ 2 marks

3. How do you know that Mindy Kim's new home has more space? Give two pieces of evidence to support your answer.

   ....
   ....
   ....

   ☐ 2 marks

4. 'CRASH!' Why do you think the writer used capital letters for this word?

   ....

   ☐ 1 mark

5. Why do you think Mindy named her favourite dog toy 'Snowball'?

   ....

   ☐ 1 mark

1 '…then he'll "consider" getting me one.' Has Dad promised that Mindy Kim can have a puppy? Explain why you think this.

....

....

2 marks

2 Find two pieces of evidence that suggest that Mindy Kim would be a good dog owner.

....

....

2 marks

3 Why do you think Dad was carrying a box of dishes?

....

....

1 mark

4 Why was Dad upset about the broken dishes?

....

....

1 mark

5 Do you think Mindy's apartment in California had a backyard? Give a reason for your answer.

....

....

2 marks

Total: _____ / 21 marks

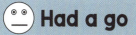 **Had a go** ☐   **Getting there** ☐   **Got it!** ☐

Taking Out The Tigers

At twilight time
or early morning
a tiger-sized ROAR
is a fearsome warning
as a huge cat swaggers
through a fine sea mist
its paws the size
of a boxer's fist,

when they're
taking out the tigers
on Sandown beach.

These tough kitties
have something to teach
about the law of the jungle
on Sandown beach.
And any kind of dog
would be most unwise
to challenge a cat
that's this sort of size,

when they're
taking out the tigers
on Sandown beach.

As a weak sun sinks
in a winter sky,
it reflects in the jewel
of a tiger's eye,
but an Indian Ocean
is dreams away
from the chilly surf
of Sandown Bay,

when they're
taking out the tigers
on Sandown beach,
taking out the tigers
on Sandown Beach,
taking out the
tigerrrrrrrrrrrs.

by Brian Moses

Challenge 1

1 'At twilight time...' What time of day is twilight?

....

2 '...a fearsome warning...' Write another word that is similar in meaning to 'fearsome'.

....

1 mark

3 What adjective is used to describe the size of the tigers?

....

1 mark

4 '...a huge cat swaggers...' Circle the word below that is closest in meaning to the word 'swaggers'.

sways   **struts**   **tiptoes**   **gallops**

1 mark

5 '...the chilly surf...' Which picture shows surf?

a.   b.   c.

1 mark

Challenge 2

1 What do you think a 'tiger-sized ROAR' would sound like?

....

1 mark

2 In what season does the poem take place?

....

1 mark

3 What kind of weather do the tigers experience on the beach?

....

1 mark

4 'taking out the tigerrrrrrrrrrs.'

Why do you think the poet has spelled 'tigerrrrrrrrrrs' this way?

....

1 mark

Challenge 3

1 '…its paws the size / of a boxer's fist.' What does this line suggest about the tiger's paws?

....

1 mark

2 What word does the poet use for the tigers that you might usually use for pet cats?

....

1 mark

3 Name two places mentioned in the poem that the tigers might have originally come from.

....

2 marks

4 '…it reflects in the jewel / of a tiger's eye…' How might a tiger's eye look like a jewel?.

....

1 mark

5 How would you feel if you saw tigers going for a walk when you were at the beach?

....

....

1 mark

Total: _____ / 15 marks

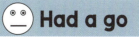 Had a go   Getting there   Got it!

What is Science?

The minute you hop out of bed in the morning, you land in the world of science.

You look at a clock, phone or computer to check the time — these devices exist because of science. You open a refrigerator to get something to eat, and the food is fresh and tasty because the refrigerator kept it cold. The refrigerator works due to science.

Your food is based in science, too. The wheat in bread was grown using science. The baking that turns raw ingredients into bread is science in action.

Science is the way humans figure out how everything in the world works. Ever since early humans lit the first campfire, chipped the first stone tools, and created the first cave paintings, we have been scientists. Our ancestors used their powers of observation to find the best way of doing these things — and then experimented to find out what kinds of materials burned — and which ones burned best. They tested rocks to find the ones that could be carved, and they looked for substances that would stick to cave walls. These are all examples of science in action.

People study science so they can work as scientists. Many scientists find ways to make new medicines, discover cures for diseases, or invent new materials.

You've probably seen scientists in movies — they usually show up in white lab coats and work in labs filled with bubbling test tubes. Many scientists really do work in laboratories, but many also work outside them — and they don't wear lab coats! Scientists can be found digging up fossils in deserts, climbing trees in rain forests, scuba diving on coral reefs, and even floating in space, tethered to a space station.

First scientists

When early humans first made fire, they also became the first scientists. They were causing a chemical reaction that released energy in the form of heat and light. Ash found in a cave in L'Escale, in south-eastern France, dates from 700,000 to 400,000 B.C, and may be the earliest remains of man-made fire.

from *Science Encyclopedia* by National Geographic Kids

Challenge 1

1. What word does the text use collectively for clocks, phones and computers? ....

1 mark

2. '...raw ingredients into bread...' Circle the word below that is closest in meaning to 'ingredients'.

    tools   **components**   **nutrients**   **science**

1 mark

3. What is one ingredient in bread that is mentioned in the text?

    ....

1 mark

4. Find one thing the text says you might see in a lab in a movie.

    ....

1 mark

5. '...tethered to a space station.' Circle the word below that is closest in meaning to the word 'tethered'.

    sent   **tied**   **bonded**   **travelling**

1 mark

Challenge 2

1. Find one modern and one ancient example of something described in the text as 'science in action'.

Modern example	
Ancient example	

2 marks

2. Based on the text, why do you think our ancestors wanted to find substances that would stick to cave walls?

    ....

1 mark

3. Find and copy the full word that 'lab' is short for.

    ....

1 mark

4. According to the text, how might the work of modern scientists benefit people?

    ....

    ....

3 marks

Challenge 3

1 'The minute you hop out of bed in the morning, you land in the world of science.' What does this sentence suggest about science?

....

1 mark

2 According to the text, how are scientists portrayed in films?

....

2 marks

3 Find another piece of evidence from the text to support the idea that our ancestors spent time in caves.

....

....

1 mark

4 Give two places other than labs where scientists work.

....

2 marks

5 Find two pieces of evidence that tell us that our ancestors used caves.

....

....

2 marks

6 Look at the different places the text tells us modern scientists might work. Which place would you most like to work, and why?

....

....

1 mark

Total: _____ / 21 marks

 Had a go □   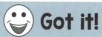 **Getting there** □   **Got it!** □

The Lion, the Witch and the Wardrobe

"Nothing there!" said Peter, and they all trooped out again – all except Lucy. She stayed behind because she thought it would be worth while trying the door of the wardrobe, even though she felt almost sure that it would be locked. To her surprise it opened quite easily, and two mothballs dropped out.

Looking into the inside, she saw several coats hanging up – mostly long fur coats. There was nothing Lucy liked so much as the smell and feel of fur. She immediately stepped into the wardrobe and got in among the coats and rubbed her face against them, leaving the door open, of course, because she knew that it is very foolish to shut oneself into any wardrobe. Soon she went further in and found that there was a second row of coats hanging up behind the first one. It was almost quite dark in there and she kept her arms stretched out in front of her so as not to bump her face into the back of the wardrobe. She took a step further in – then two or three steps – always expecting to feel woodwork against the tips of her fingers. But she could not feel it.

"This must be a simply enormous wardrobe!" thought Lucy, going still further in and pushing the soft folds of the coats aside to make room for her. Then she noticed that there was something crunching under her feet. "I wonder is that more mothballs?" she thought, stooping down to feel it with her hand. But instead of feeling the hard, smooth wood of the floor of the wardrobe, she felt something soft and powdery and extremely cold. "This is very queer," she said, and went on a step or two further.

Next moment she found that what was rubbing against her face and hands was no longer soft fur but something hard and rough and even prickly. "Why, it is just like branches of trees!" exclaimed Lucy. And then she saw that there was a light ahead of her; not a few inches away where the back of the wardrobe ought to have been, but a long way off. Something cold and soft was falling on her. A moment later she found that was standing in the middle of a wood at night-time with snow under her feet and snowflakes falling through the air.

by C.S. Lewis

Challenge 1

1 '…they all trooped out again…' Circle the word below that is closest in meaning to 'trooped'.

ran   fled   marched   came

1 mark

2 Apart from Lucy, what other person is named in the text?

1 mark

3 '…it is very foolish to shut oneself into any wardrobe.' Write another word that is similar in meaning to 'foolish'.

1 mark

4 Find and copy two adjectives used to describe the wood of the floor of the wardrobe.

2 marks

5 What does Lucy find hanging behind the first row of coats?

1 mark

Challenge 2

1 Why was Lucy surprised when the wardrobe door opened?

1 mark

2 Why did Lucy climb into the wardrobe?

1 mark

3 Why should you not shut yourself in any wardrobe?

1 mark

4 What other action did Lucy take to keep herself safe in the wardrobe?

1 mark

5 What two things is the adjective 'soft' used to describe in the text?

....

2 marks

Challenge 3

1 Why do you think Lucy decides the wardrobe must be 'simply enormous'?

....

....

1 mark

2 '…she felt something soft and powdery and extremely cold.'
What do you think Lucy felt on the floor of the wardrobe?

....

1 mark

3 'This is very queer…' What does this sentence suggest about how Lucy is feeling at this point? Include two ideas.

....

....

2 marks

4 What do you think will happen next in the story? Give a reason for your answer.

....

....

2 marks

Total: _____ / 18 marks

 Had a go ☐   **Getting there** ☐   😄 **Got it!** ☐

Progress Test 3

Working in Space

We have all seen workers on a construction site, hammering and drilling. Imagine a construction site travelling in space high above the Earth's surface. That's what astronauts have to cope with when they are repairing a satellite, or putting together a space station.

Is it warm today?

In orbit, the strong sunshine heats astronauts up. Surprisingly, it's difficult to lose heat in space, so spacesuits have to include a refrigeration unit!

Hands on

Astronauts say that moving their hands in their gloves is difficult. To feel what they mean, put a rubber band around your closed fingers and try to open them. Do this 15 times.

Make it larger

Space tools are extra large so that astronauts can grab them in their bulky gloves. They also have to be tied to the astronaut to prevent them from floating away.

Slow down

Astronauts have to work slower than construction workers on the Earth. If they twist a bolt too quickly, they will send themselves into a spin.

A piece of history

The first-ever spacewalk was performed by Soviet astronaut Alexi Leonov on 18 March 1965. He was soon followed by American Edward White on 3 June 1965.

1. **Find two jobs that astronauts might do in space.**

   ....

   2 marks

2. **What adjective is used to decsribe astronauts' gloves?**

   ....

   1 mark

3. **Would astronauts be able to use Earth tools in space? Give a reason for your answer.**

   ....

   ....

   2 marks

4. **What would happen if the refrigeration unit in an astronaut's suit stopped working?**

   ....

   1 mark

5. **Which section gives information about the early spacewalks?**

   ....

   1 mark

6. **What could you do to see what it feels like to wear astronaut's gloves?**

   ....

   ....

   1 mark

7. **Find one possible danger an astronaut might face when working in space.**

   ....

   ....

   1 mark

Nim's Island by Wendy Orr

IN A PALM TREE, on an island, in the middle of the wide blue sea, was a girl.

Nim's hair was wild, her eyes were bright, and around her neck she wore three cords. One was for a spyglass, one for a whirly, whistling shell and the other a fat, red pocket-knife in a sheath.

With the spyglass at her eye, she watched her father's boat. It sailed out through the reef to the deeper dark ocean, and Jack turned to wave and Nim waved back, though she knew he couldn't see.

Then the white sails caught the wind and blew him out of sight, and Nim was alone. For three days and three nights, whatever happened or needed doing, Nim would do it.

'And what we need first,' said Nim, 'is breakfast!' So she threw four ripe coconuts *thump!* into the sand, and climbed down after them.

Then she whistled her shell, two long, shrill notes that carried far out to the reef where sea lions were fishing. Selkie popped her head above the water. She had a fish in her mouth, but she swallowed it fast and dived towards the beach.

8. How does the first sentence set the scene for the story?

....

....

2 marks

9. Why can Nim see her father when he waves, but he cannot see her? ....

....

1 mark

10. How is Nim's father's boat powered? ....

1 mark

11. What does Nim do that suggests she isn't worried about being left alone?

....

1 mark

12. '*thump!*' Why do you think the writer put this word in italics?

....

1 mark

13. '...two long, shrill notes...' Write another word that is similar in meaning to 'shrill'.

....

1 mark

14. Who or what do you think Selkie is? Give a reason for your answer.

....

....

2 marks

15. Why do you think Nim whistles her shell?

....

1 mark

Total: _____ / 19 marks

Answers

Pages 6–11 Starter Test

1.

merry	→ riches
giant	→ good
treasure	→ huge
beautiful	→ jolly
kind	→ attractive

(merry → jolly, giant → huge, treasure → riches, beautiful → attractive, kind → good) **[5]**

2. a castle, a fairy, a witch, a princess **[4]**
3. Page 11 **[1]** 4. Basketball **[1]**
5. three pages **[1]** 6. Rugby **[1]**
7. Accept any answer supported by a reason. **[1]**
8. raining **[1]** 9. circus **[1]**
10. train **[1]** 11. large **[1]** 12. funny **[1]**
13. pink **[1]** 14. shiny red **[1]**

15.	At the zoo	elephant	tiger	camel
16.	At the playground	swings	slide	roundabout
17.	In the living room	television	sofa	chair

[9]

18. to 20. Accept any answers which make sense, e.g. chocolate, birthday. **[1]**; train, bus **[1]**; crossed **[1]**.
21. very small **[1]** 22. carefully **[1]**
23. breakfast **[1]**
24. Because someone is bringing his breakfast upstairs to him. **[1]**
25. One from: food / drink packaging, toys, clothes, magazines, cardboard boxes, plastic bottles. **[1]**
26. outgrown **[1]** 27. recycle it **[1]**
28. new bottles, fleece clothing **[2]**
29. They do not play with them anymore. **[1]**
30. wood **[1]** 31. bank **[1]**
32. A child **[1]**. Reasons might vary, e.g. because children like to play on the beach. **[1]**
33. Accept any answer which makes sense, e.g. the narrator's parents. **[1]**
34. because they were full of water **[1]**
35. webbed **[1]** 36. 327 years old **[1]**
37. Accept any word with a similar meaning to 'jersey', e.g. jumper, sweater. **[1]**
38. The Martian is feeling worried or afraid **[1]**, and we know this because the text describes him as 'nervous'. (Children may also identify that shivering could also suggest that he is worried or afraid.) **[1]**
39. The Martian had not landed on Earth before **[1]**, because to him everything looked 'strange and frightening'. **[1]**

Pages 14–15

Challenge 1
1. huddled **[1]** 2. gigantic, great wings **[2]**
3. They were very upset. **[1]**

Challenge 2
1. sheep, goats, chickens **[1]**
2. It was too quick for them. **[1]**
3. in storehouses and granaries **[2]**

Challenge 3
1. The villagers cannot grow food in the winter, so they need to store food grown in the summer. **[1]**
2. Because it was hidden by the thick canopy of leaves. **[1]**
3. The villagers would not have seen the bird at night because they would be sleeping / it would be too dark. **[2]**

Pages 16–17

Challenge 1
1. blue **[1]** 2. sleepy **[1]** 3. summer **[1]**

Challenge 2
1. sat on my hand; lit on my fingers **[2]**
2. wings like spun glass **[1]** 3. on grass **[1]**

Challenge 3
1. it was drowsy; it thought the hand was grass **[2]**
2. 'Made drowsy the land' **[1]**
3. Answers will vary, e.g. The narrator admires the dragonfly's beauty. **[1]**

Pages 18–19

Challenge 1
1. grey **[1]** 2. 'They vary in size' **[1]**
3. a) True, b) False, c) False, d) False **[4]**

Challenge 2
1. Kodiak bear **[1]** 2. in the Middle East **[1]**
3. 15 **[1]**

Challenge 3
1. Kodiak bear / Alaskan brown bear **[2]**
2. No, because the fact they only 'tend' to be light in colour suggests some are not. **[2]**
3. Accept any reasonable answer, e.g. bears live in many different places so it would be difficult to find and count them all. **[1]**

Pages 20–21

Challenge 1
1. mixture **[1]** 2. two o'clock **[1]** 3. a) True, b) False, c) True, d) True **[4]**

Challenge 2
1. Two from: cakes, jams, pickles, preserves. **[2]**
2. energy, words **[2]**
3. 'quiet valley below the farm' **[1]**

Challenge 3
1. Any two from: she refers to the sound as 'a racket' / 'a row', she says it sounds like someone being murdered. **[2]**

2. it is a 'usually quiet valley' [1]
3. Because they are excited. [1]

Pages 22–23
Challenge 1
1. splendid [1] 2. silver [1] 3. gleaming [1]
Challenge 2
1. white, red [2] 2. the river, the well [2]
3. 'He resembles the rainbow.' [1]
Challenge 3
1. Answers will vary, e.g. The narrator thinks the bull is magnificent [1] because she/he compares him to beautiful things in nature. The narrator seems to idolise and adore the bull because she/he praises him throughout the poem and calls him 'my bull'. [1]
2. Answers will vary, e.g. It reflects the contrasting light and dark colourings of the bull. [1]
3. The narrator thinks the water is better in the river, and wants the best for the bull, and that is why she/he is prepared to use her/his spear to drive away her/his enemies. [1]

Pages 24–25
Challenge 1
1. knocking [1] 2. skeletal [1]
3. Madagascar [1]
Challenge 2
1. It is nocturnal and it has a special middle finger. [2]
2. coconuts and other fruit [2]
3. They help it see in low light. [1]
Challenge 3
1. To find food grown by humans. [1]
2. No, because aye-ayes do not hurt people and are 'gentle'. [2]
3. Accept creatures or animals. [1]

Pages 26–27
Challenge 1
1. alarm [1] 2. frock [1] 3. red [1]
Challenge 2
1. To draw attention to it [1] and to reinforce the idea that Bill has not worn a dress before. [1]
2. Because he can't believe what he is seeing. [1]
3. a) The word 'swept' suggests she is moving quickly [1]. b) She is moving like this because she is late [1].
Challenge 3
1. No [1], because they both react as though it's perfectly normal – his mother suggests he wears a dress and his father tells him he looks sweet, as if they are used to him being a girl. [1]

2. He has become angry. [1]
3. Accept any reasonable answer [1], supported by an explanation [1], e.g. Bill has to go to school in the dress, but nobody there mentions that he used to be a boy either.

Pages 28–29
Challenge 1
1. verify [1] 2. everybody [1]
3. Any word with a similar meaning to 'rubble', e.g. wreckage or ruins. [1]
Challenge 2
1. No [1], because the narrator says that 'every great success' comes after making mistakes. [1]
2. 'countless hours of trouble' [1]
3. Because you remember what you learn from mistakes. [1]
Challenge 3
1. Mistakes are an opportunity to learn [1] and people might have to make many mistakes before they succeed [1].

Pages 30–31
Challenge 1
1. the giant redwood [1] 2. tropical forests [1] 3. North America [1]
Challenge 2
1. giants, large (also accept impressive) [2]
2. They move gracefully and/or quietly. [1]
3. agile [1]
Challenge 3
1. No, because they change colour to match their surroundings. [2]
2. So they can creep up on their prey. [1]
3. Accept any answer [1] supported by a reason. [1]

Pages 32–35 Progress Test 1
1. The narrator is the character who tells the story. [1]
2. The narrator is a child [1] because he/she talks about being at school now ('He only joined our class last year...') [1].
3. a word that gives more information about a noun [1]
4. smallest, funniest [2] 5. Michael [1]
6.

Tom	Accept one from: he is funny; he can eat a lot.
Josie	Accept one from: she is fast and good at football; she is cool.

[2]

7. He thinks Tom will eat them because he is always hungry. [1]

91

8. No, because you could not fit a million freckles on someone's face. **[2]**
9. 'a shimmer of glass' **[1]**
10. remains **[1]**
11. **a)** False, **b)** False, **c)** True, **d)** True **[4]**
12. A long time **[1]** because the children have grown up, or because the school has become a ruin, or because the school has been forgotten **[1]**.
13. Two from: 'as the night draws in and the dark descends', 'as the night draws on', 'as the night creeps up to the edge of the day'. **[2]**
14. Answers may vary, e.g. because the sun is rising / daylight is coming. **[1]**

Pages 36–38
Challenge 1
1. bear **[1]**   2. eleven years old **[1]**
3. **a)** True, **b)** True, **c)** False, **d)** False **[4]**
Challenge 2
1. 'next to ours' **[1]**   2. 'Every time I went over to their farm' **[1]**
3. It has been shot and killed by the Gregg family **[1]** because they carry the deer out of the woods, and the text says that they go into the woods to hunt. **[1]**
4. It draws the readers' attention to it and makes it more dramatic. **[1]**
Challenge 3
1. Mr Gregg's behaviour suggests he does not care what the narrator thinks and does not want to listen to her. **[1]**
2. 'Every Sunday morning they would take their guns and go off into the woods to look for animals and birds to shoot.' 'Then, one Saturday morning, I saw Philip and William coming out of the woods with their father, and they were carrying a lovely young deer.' **[2]**
3. Answers will vary, e.g. putting the magic finger on the Gregg family will cause something funny and dramatic to happen to them, to teach them a lesson. **[1]**

Pages 39–41
Challenge 1
1. scowl **[1]**   2. pleased **[1]**
3. Three from: calm down, stop, be quiet, eat, sleep **[3]**   4. bad, glad **[2]**
Challenge 2
1. 'If you're sad then I don't care' **[1]**
2. To help them to calm down and go to sleep. **[1]**
3. To suggest that the narrator's shouting is getting louder. **[1]**

4. To suggest that the narrator is feeling very angry at this point in the poem. **[1]**
Challenge 3
1. Answers will vary, e.g. I think the narrator would bite someone **[1]** because they are so angry **[1]**. / I do not think the narrator would really bite someone **[1]** because biting is very wrong **[1]**. / I do not think the narrator would really bite someone **[1]** as they only said that because they were so angry. **[1]**
2. A riot is usually a violent act by a group of people, so if one person is like a riot, they must be making a lot of noise and disturbance **[1]**. Using capital letters for the word 'riot' draws attention to this idea **[1]**.
3. The narrator suddenly loses their anger and feels ready to be calm. **[1]**

Pages 42–44
Challenge 1
1. Any word with a similar meaning to 'gigantic', e.g. huge, massive, enormous. **[1]**
2. Incredible **[1]**   3. Africa is divided into 55 countries **[1]**   4. villages, shanty-towns **[2]**
Challenge 2
1. To draw attention to it and highlight how much the writer admires Africa. **[1]**
2. To show surprise and admiration at the size of Africa. **[1]**
3. To show how much people in Africa study. **[1]**
4. 'hot, blinding deserts', 'cold, snowy mountains'. **[2]**
5. Any one of: dark, dripping; camels and Coca-Cola; Lamborghinis and lions; singing and smiling **[1]**
Challenge 3
1. No **[1]**, the text is just explaining that our ancestors did. **[1]**
2. It suggests that the way Africa is divided into countries could change. **[1]**
3. Accept any sensible answer, e.g. there is snow in Africa. **[1]**
4. Because the lush foliage blocks out the sunshine. **[1]**

Pages 45–47
Challenge 1
1. winter **[1]**   2. Thomas and Pete **[1]**
3. argument **[1]**   4. commotion **[1]**
Challenge 2
1. To reinforce the idea that Melanie cries easily. **[1]**
2. No **[1]**, because they are in a bad temper **[1]**.
3. grumbled, muttered **[2]**

4. they groan **[1]**

5. Closed **[1]** because each class would have its own teacher / would be learning different things **[1]**.

Challenge 3

1. Accept any description that shows he is not a nice person e.g. 'was trying to pick a quarrel' **[1]** and is often in trouble, e.g. 'just [wanted] to be a nuisance as usual' **[1]**.

2. Because something unexpected has happened **[1]** and the children are surprised **[1]**.

3. Answers may vary, e.g. it suggests something magical is about to happen. **[1]** 4. 'and all that sort of stuff' **[1]**

Pages 48–50
Challenge 1

1. Any word with a similar meaning to 'casket', e.g. box or chest **[1]**

2. Shabby **[1]** 3. red **[1]** 4. dragon, unicorn, mermaid **[3]** 5. Ancient **[1]**

Challenge 2

1. She might live in a castle. **[1]**

2. No **[1]**, because statues cannot cry **[1]**.

3. Two from: patterns stolen by the sun / faded; fringes frayed; tufts flattened **[2]**

4. Its patterns had been stolen by the desert sun. **[1]**

5. It suggests it moves like water. **[1]**

Challenge 3

1. Because birdsong sounds nice. **[1]**

2. Two from: it had been faded by the desert sun, frayed by ice storms, flattened by sleeping tigers; it smelt of spices, meadow flowers and salty seas. **[2]**

3. A flying carpet **[1]** because it travels to different places / the poet says it moves across the room like a flying fish **[1]**.

4. Accept any sensible answer **[1]** supported by a reason **[1]**.

Pages 51–53
Challenge 1

1. One from: fuel, oxygen, heat **[1]**

2. chemical **[1]** 3. light **[1]** 4. Accept any word with a similar meaning to 'source', e.g. get, obtain, find. **[1]**

Challenge 2

1. wood **[1]**

2. No **[1]**, because the text says you must have all three basic ingredients to make fire start. **[1]**

3. Because matches can be dangerous. **[1]**

4. Because you might need to put out a fire. **[1]**

5. It is a dried out version / It has a lower water content. **[1]**

Challenge 3

1. No **[1]**. The text says that kindling burns well because it is dry, which suggests wet things will not burn well. **[1]**

2. 4. Combustion. **[1]**

3. To make sure the fire cannot spread to the surrounding area. **[1]**

4. Because it is easier/quicker than rubbing sticks together. **[1]**

5. Answers should refer to either lightning or a volcano creating heat that ignites the fuel (for example kindling or wood), and the reaction between the fuel and oxygen in the air causing the fuel to burn. **[3]**

Pages 54–57 Progress Test 2

1. squirrel, bird **[2]**

2. a kite **[1]**

3. In summer, trees have leaves so it is like they are 'clothed'. In winter, trees have lost their leaves so they are 'bare'. **[1]**

4. Because he/she is asleep at night. **[1]**

5. Because the moon has existed for a very long time. **[1]**

6. He thinks they are generous and love to give. **[1]**

7. No, because the tree offers so much, but we just cut them down and burn them. **[2]**

8. 'changed her life forever', 'would never walk again' **[2]**

9. she felt very sad / unhappy / depressed **[1]**

10. Pakistan **[1]**

11. Because it is an unusual word and it is important that readers understand what it means. **[1]**

12. Her paralysis made it difficult to know whether she was too cold. **[1]**

13. Children should identify that the writer thinks Darke will continue to achieve amazing things because she is described as 'unstoppable', and her 'abilities seem to know no limits'. **[2]**

14. Accept any reasonable answer, supported with a reason. **[2]**

Pages 58–61
Challenge 1

1. agreeable **[1]** 2. Stuart **[1]**
3. shocked **[1]** 4. a park **[1]** 5. jolt **[1]**

Challenge 2

1. No, because the text says he was 'agreeable' about helping out **[1]** and he doesn't mind going down the drain **[1]**.

93

2. Answers may vary, e.g. the ring might have been valuable and / or a gift. **[1]**

3. It was dark in the drain so she couldn't see, the hook got caught, the ring was too far down. **[3]**

4. Because he thinks it will be wet down the drain and he doesn't mind getting his old pants wet. **[1]**

Challenge 3

1. No **[1]**, because the text says Stuart helps his parents and his brother to do things that only a mouse can do, and George would not need this help if he were small too. **[1]**

2. It was his idea and he wanted to be the one to help get the ring back. **[1]**

3. It would be dark ('it was dark down the drain') and wet ('I imagine it's wet down there'). **[2]**

4. Relieved that Stuart was back safely **[1]** and happy to have the ring back **[1]**.

Page 62–65

Challenge 1

1. fake **[1]** 2. in the middle of the night / late at night **[1]** 3. shouted very loudly **[1]** 4. make sure **[1]** 5. morning **[1]**

Challenge 2

1. He wants us to feel sorry for her. **[1]**

2. Exclamation marks can be used to show emotion, so they show that Cinderella is excited / desperate. **[1]**

3. 'And quickly, in no time at all' **[1]**

4. To show that he grabbed the slipper very quickly, because darts move very quickly. **[1]**

Challenge 3

1. Because the 'real' version was too scary for children. **[1]**

2. So she could not go to the ball **[1]**, and because they wanted to put her somewhere horrible **[1]**.

3. They were jealous / annoyed **[1]**; the poet uses the word 'wince' to show how painful they found the sight **[1]**.

4. He is in love with Cinderella and people say that makes your heart beat faster. **[1]**

Pages 66–69

Challenge 1

1. ancient **[1]** 2. London **[1]** 3. University of Cambridge **[1]** 4. strange **[1]**

5. 200 million years ago **[1]**

Challenge 2

1. palaeontologist **[1]**

2. There were many fossils there. **[1]**

3. The ammonite **[1]**; its living relatives are the octopus, squid and cuttlefish. **[1]**

4. The Ichthyosaur probably had large eyes to help it see better underwater. **[1]**

5. She sold them to make money which she might have shared with her family. **[1]**

Challenge 3

1. Because there had been no evidence of these animals until Anning found their fossilised remains. **[1]**

2. He bought fossils from her. **[1]**

3. Women weren't treated as well as men / weren't considered as important as men. **[1]**

4. When she was alive, she was not given all of the credit for her work, but now we know that she changed the way we see the world. **[1]**

5. Accept any sensible answer, e.g. To help it to hunt / To help it to see predators coming. **[1]**

Pages 70–73

Challenge 1

1. California **[1]**

2. Accept any word with a similar meaning to 'convince', e.g. persuade. **[1]**

3. Thirteen **[1]**

4. lots of outdoor space to run **[1]**

5. sensible **[1]**

Challenge 2

1. How to take care of puppies; huskies. **[2]**

2. She looks at a website about them ('looking through a website on huskies, one of my *favorite* kinds of dogs') and has a stuffed husky toy. **[2]**

3. It has a backyard which they didn't have before, and she says their old kitchen was smaller. **[2]**

4. To highlight how loud the sound was. **[1]**

5. Because it is white. **[1]**

Challenge 3

1. No **[1]**, because 'consider' means he will think about but it, but he has not promised **[1]**.

2. She has found out what puppies need **[1]** and understands that it would not have been right to have had one in their apartment **[1]**.

3. They are unpacking because they have moved house. **[1]**

4. Because Mindy Kim's mother had liked them, and she has now died. **[1]**

5. No **[1]**, because Mindy says that now they have a backyard they can have a puppy, which suggests they didn't have a yard before **[1]**.

Pages 74–77

Challenge 1

1. evening / dusk **[1]**

2. Accept any word with a similar meaning to 'fearsome', e.g. scary, frightening. **[1]**

3. huge **[1]**   4. struts **[1]**   5. c) **[1]**

Challenge 2

1. It would be big and loud, because tigers are big animals. **[1]**
2. winter **[1]**   3. sea mist **[1]**
4. because when you say it out loud, the word sounds like a tiger growling. **[1]**

Challenge 3

1. It suggests their paws are very large because a boxer wears big gloves on their fists which makes them look huge **[1]**.
2. kitties **[1]**
3. the jungle, Indian Ocean **[2]**
4. Accept any reasonable answer, e.g. reference to shininess or colour.
5. Accept any sensible answer, e.g. I would feel afraid because tigers are dangerous. **[1]**

Pages 78–81

Challenge 1

1. devices **[1]**   2. components **[1]**
3. wheat **[1]**   4. bubbling test tubes **[1]**
5. tied **[1]**

Challenge 2

1.
Modern example	Baking bread
Ancient example	Accept one of the following: experimenting to see what would burn; testing rocks to find ones to carve; looking for substances that would stick to cave walls.

     [2]

2. Because they wanted to make cave paintings. **[1]**
3. laboratory **[1]**
4. They might make new medicines, discover cures for diseases or invent new materials. **[3]**

Challenge 3

1. Science is all around us. **[1]**
2. working in labs and wearing lab coats **[2]**
3. Ash was found in a cave in France. **[1]**
4. Two from: in deserts, rain forests, coral reefs or space. **[2]**
5. The text mentions cave paintings and ash from a man-made fire that was found in a cave. **[2]**
6. Accept any choice that is supported with a reason. **[1]**

Pages 82–85

Challenge 1

1. marched **[1]**

2. Peter **[1]**
3. Any word with a similar meaning to 'foolish', e.g. silly / unwise. **[1]**
4. hard and smooth **[2]**
5. another row of coats **[1]**

Challenge 2

1. She expected it to be locked. **[1]**
2. She wanted to smell and feel the fur coats. **[1]**
3. You might not be able to open the door from the inside and would be trapped. **[1]**
4. She put her hands out in front of her so she wouldn't walk into the back of the wardrobe and injure herself. **[1]**
5. the coats and the snow **[2]**

Challenge 3

1. because she keeps walking but does not reach the back **[1]**
2. snow **[1]**
3. She is very confused **[1]**, because she expects to bend down and touch the wooden floor of the wardrobe **[1]**.
4. Accept any reasonable answer, e.g. she will explore the wood. **[2]**

Pages 86–89 Progress Test 3

1. repairing a satellite, putting together a space station **[2]**
2. bulky **[1]**
3. No **[1]**, because they would not be able to grip them in their bulky gloves. **[1]**
4. The astronaut would get very hot. **[1]**
5. 'A piece of history' **[1]**
6. You could put an elastic band around your closed fingers and try to open them. **[1]**
7. If they turned a bolt too quickly, they could send themselves into a spin. **[1]**
8. It tells the reader that the story takes place on an island **[1]**, and introduces the reader to the main character, Nim **[1]**.
9. Nim is looking through her spyglass so she can see objects in the distance. **[1]**
10. by a sail **[1]**
11. She starts to prepare for breakfast. **[1]**
12. To draw attention to the sound of the coconuts hitting the ground. **[1]**
13. Accept any word with a similar meaning to 'shrill', e.g. high, sharp, piercing. **[1]**
14. A sea lion, because she is where the sea lions fish, and she has a fish in her mouth. **[2]**
15. To call Selkie to her. **[1]**

Fill in your score for each progress test in the window of the rocket.

Progress
Test 1

Progress
Test 2

Progress
Test 3